I am a red dress

I am a red dress

INCANTATIONS ON

A GRANDMOTHER,

A MOTHER,

AND A DAUGHTER

Anna Camilleri

ARSENAL PULP PRESS
Vancouver

Arsenal Pulp Press
103 – 1014 Homer Street
Vancouver, B.C.
Canada v6b 2w9
arsenalpulp.com

The publisher gratefully acknowledges the support of the Canada Council for the Arts and the British Columbia Arts Council for its publishing program, and the Government of Canada through the Book Publishing Industry Development Program for its publishing activities.

Design by Solo
Front cover photograph by R. Kelly Clipperton
Back cover and title page print by Anna Camilleri

Printed and bound in Canada

Library and Archives Canada
Cataloguing in Publication
    Camilleri, Anna
        I am a red dress : incantations on a grandmother, a mother, and a
        daughter / Anna Camilleri.
    ISBN 1-55152-163-6
        1. Title.
    PS8605.A44I35 2004   c818.6   C2004-902948-7

Dedication

Contents

Daughter

There is a vitality, a life force, a quickening
that is translated through you into action, and
because there is only one of you in all time,
this expression is unique. And if you block it,
it will never exist through any other medium
and [will] be lost. The world will not have it.

It is not your business to determine how
good it is; nor how it compares with other
expressions. It is your business to keep it yours,
clearly and directly, to keep the channel open.

You do not even have to believe in yourself or your work. You have to keep open and aware directly to the urge that motivates you. Keep the channel open.

No artist is pleased. There is no satisfaction whatever at any time. There is only a queer, divine dissatisfaction, a blessed unrest that keeps us marching and makes us more alive than the others.

— MARTHA GRAHAM TO AGNES DE MILLE

Prologue

My mother often said, "When your grandfather dies, I'm going to the funeral in a red dress."

Sometimes this declaration was preceded by a long string of curses, sometimes it emerged as a single thought bubble that evaporated as quickly as it came. This sentence – along with the flash in my mother's eyes, the red blush at her neck, a smack upon the kitchen counter or a door slammed shut – more than any other memory, or experience, characterized my girlhood, and set the stage for the woman I would later become.

When he dies, I'm going to the funeral in a red dress was said so frequently, it became a prayer, a lullaby, an incantation – something I expected, like Sunday lunch at my grandmother's house.

Still life: Toronto, 1975. We're all sitting around the kitchen table. My grandmother Anna is taking the picture, but if someone else was, she still wouldn't be in it; she'd be busy eating from the pot in between washing dishes and making sauce for next Sunday's lunch. I'm sitting on my uncle Fabrizio's lap. We both have red hair that turns light brown; mine is in pigtails, and his is frizzy to his shoulders. My eyes are blue in this picture; sometimes they're grey, but mostly green. We call him Fab for short; he is the youngest of my mother's three brothers. My uncle Domenic and my uncle Mike, wearing shiny polyester shirts, look bored. To the right, there's my dad and my mom with my baby brother Johnny on her lap. My parents look like movie stars. My dad wears a light blue cotton shirt and has bushy sideburns to the middle of his face. My mom is so pretty with her long hair and dimples. My grandfather Ernesto is sitting next to her. He's not looking at my grandmother when the camera goes click. He's looking at me. After the table has been cleared and my grandfather has gone out, my mother says, *When he dies, I'm going to the funeral in a red dress.* My grandmother looks at her, but doesn't say anything.

My grandfather is a character in this story, but he is not the subject. He is at the edge of the photograph, at the seams of the story where the fabric divides, threatening to come undone. The real story is everything between the seams; the flow of fabric taut across round of belly; the moment of entry; a woman wearing a red dress walks into a room, into a dream, onto a stage, the sway of cloth against a suggestion of legs, long and strong; of women painting themselves red; of me painting myself red – what this does, and might mean.

This story is a lexicon between my grandmother, my mother, and I – the stuff that mythology is made of – mother, maiden, and crone. Grandmother notices a red dress. Mother imagines wearing a red dress. Daughter becomes the red dress. The redress.

Grand-
mother

why are there no silences? we desire nothing

so much as a perfect long black silence. but life

is filled with noise. I suspect that death too is

noisy. what is the yearning for silence? perhaps

it is the rock in me, the ancient lava, the sea

floor, the hardness and roundness of my skull

like a boulder, the sea salt in my blood, the

salty blood in motion like the sea.

— LIBBY SCHEIER

Lexicon of the Red Dress, part 1

My grandmother Anna wasn't a beauty queen, but I thought she was more beautiful than anyone in any glossy magazine. The skin under her neck and across her chest was as soft and delicate as sifted flour. Her chestnut-brown hair, clipped into a roll at the back of her head for as long as I remember, was just on the other side of tidy; a starburst of loose hairs fluttering about her face like bees in search of pollen. She wore makeup only on very rare occasions: a stripe of pale pink across her lips; foundation, spread only on the right side of her face, over top of the wine-coloured birthmark that stretched from her widow's peak to the nape of her neck. My grandmother often said, "God didn't make me beautiful, but he made me strong as an ox." When I was a little girl, I used to reach for the crimson skin on her face, but she would wave my hand away with a cluck of her tongue: "No, no, *Annee*, it's bad – it's bad luck to touch." In the few photographs she is in, there is barely a trace of her; my grandmother is standing sideways, her bad side hidden from view.

Because of my grandmother's birthmark and the folk

mythology in Mirabella Eclano, Avellino, a small farming community south of Naples, the villagers believed her to be cursed by the devil himself. My grandmother's sisters and brother were sent to school intermittently, but my grandmother was kept behind to work the fields. *What was a cursed girl going to do with an education?* It was that same sentiment that produced her arranged marriage. My grandfather Ernesto wasn't considered a catch – as a young man, he was known to be a lazy philanderer – but any man was thought to better than no man at all.

Still life: Italy, 1951. The year of my grandparents' marriage. My grandfather and a group of army mates are posing – huddled together with arms thrown around each other. The heavily creased print looks like a sheet of wax paper that has been crumpled and then opened again. The bottom right hand corner, where my grandfather is pictured, is crease-free. I remember him as a sunken-cheeked, skinny man with pants bunched at his waist, but this photograph tells a different story. He is thick across the shoulders and chest, his chiselled jaw comes to a point in a deep cleft, blond hair swept back, blue eyes squinting at the photographer. He is a strapping twenty-two-year-old man.

A year after that photo was taken, my mother Vierra was born. I recall my grandmother saying that the only thing my grandfather was around for, from beginning to end, was their children's conception, and their voyage to Canada. It wasn't a complaint; my grandmother was setting the table for my mother's birth story.

I am a red dress

My grandfather, a cook in the Italian army, took a leave from his station for the birth of his first child; he was under strict orders to return to his post, with documentation in hand, as soon as the child was born. Having arrived a few days prior to the birth of my mother on April 11, 1952, he was due back that same day. Instead, he went on a two day drinking tear, and changed the date on my mother's birth certificate to April 13. Everyone in my family except me recognizes April 13 as my mother's birthday.

In 1954, my grandparents and my mother made the journey to Canada, by way of boat to Halifax, Nova Scotia's Pier 21. There, in the dead of winter, they boarded a train for northern Saskatchewan. They were the only Italians for miles around. My grandmother had heard from another farmhand that there was plenty of factory work in Toronto. Their time in Saskatchewan was short-lived.

In Toronto, they settled in the Dufferin/St Clair area, a working-class Italian enclave. My grandmother became a full-time factory worker with sole responsibility for a family that rapidly grew to include four children. My grandfather was often gone, usually to one of the neighbourhood billiard halls on St Clair Avenue, or drinking in the *cantina* – the cellar. His absence was noticed, as was the absence of the steady income that he could have brought into the house, but it wasn't lamented by his family. As far as they were concerned, the best thing my grandfather could do was be gone, and stay gone.

By all accounts, my grandfather Ernesto was not a kind

man, and not what you might call a decent man. He didn't treat my grandmother or their children with care. He didn't show any interest in them at all. But my grandmother Anna used to say that God had a plan, that God had a way of balancing the scales, that those who suffer would be recognized for their suffering. She vested herself in the belief that there would be some ultimate justice in death. Her body ached from long work days at the garment factory; I suspect just being free of it would have been reason enough to believe in God's plan.

Crimson Queen

Each summer, my grandmother called her children and grandchildren together. In a caravan of noisy, rust-patched cars, we drove to a farm north of Toronto where we picked tomatoes, red peppers, and eggplant. My grandmother was the happiest on these days, singing, *"La campagnola bella, tu sei la reginella, nell' occhi tuoi ce l' sole, ce l' colore* – Beautiful farm girl, you are the queen, in your eyes there is sun, colour."

The longer we drove, the smaller the buildings became; the city blew past us like a grey sheet on a bowed clothesline, and soon the air was tart with freshly laid manure. My little brother Johnny and I pinched our noses tight and tried to pull each other's hand away while clutching onto pieces of bread with our free hands. I was two years older, and bigger, so I won most of our matches.

Those drives to the farm were my favourite days. Johnny and I liked to chirp back my grandmother's song, *"Tu sei la reginella, la campagnola bella"* in round, *"Ce l' colore, ce l' sole, nell occhi tuoi . . ."* out of order. My grandmother smiled and knotted up the bottom of her blouse, wiped crumbs from my face, and tousled my brother's straight hair that he wore, by no choice of his own, in a salad bowl-special haircut until he was twelve years old. His long legs looked especially lanky because of knee-high socks.

We tumbled out of the cars, sweaty before the work had even begun, Johnny and I excited at the novelty of a day of picking. My grandmother walked ahead of us, kicked off her shoes, and wriggled her toes in the earth. Hands square on her round hips, her head tilted back, looking up at the hazy August sky – I knew she was smiling. When the farmer approached, he'd only nod at us, but address my nonna directly: *"Ciao, Signora!"*

Before he could butter her up, she launched into business: picked the greenest patch of field and agreed upon the price per bushel. We followed her like sheep. She was the queen, training our hands and eyes to select the right vegetables.

I never wandered far from her. Once, I asked, "Nonna, why don't we buy our vegetables from the store?"

"Cossi, this way, everything we eat is chosen with love and care, *Annina."* I loved when she'd call me *Annee* – pronounced *Unnee* – or *Annina.*

I squatted in the field, chewing my lower lip – which I was not allowed to do around the adults – and just watched her. God, she was fast. I wondered if the tomatoes we picked were different from any others. I decided they were because my grandmother had said so. I wondered if she meant to say that there is not enough love to go around; that it needs to be guarded, that it is rare. Despite her joy on those days, I felt Nonna's heavy heart, and I hoped that a broken heart could be repaired.

I am a red dress

On the drive back into the city, we were all quiet, leaning against the windows and each other, drifting in and out of sleep or snoring outright. All, that is, but my grandmother, who was wide awake.

At home, the vegetables were carefully unloaded onto large plastic drop sheets in my grandmother's garage. My grandmother checked them daily, gingerly picking out those with wormholes. In mid-September, it was time. My nonna announced, "The vegetables are ready – *andiamo*, let's go!" and we gathered for days of canning.

In the backyard, a large metal drum was filled with water and set down on the fire. Three hundred mason jars were washed, and a few leaves of basilica were placed at the bottom of each. Aunts, uncles, cousins, and people I called *Zia* and *Zio* (who weren't blood relations) arrived with aprons, sharp knives, and a change of clothes in tow.

My job – the job that no one else did – was to fill a small basket with twenty or so tomatoes, and hand it to my father to dunk in the drum. Nonna promoted me to cutter when I was about ten years old; I got to lop off the ends of the tomatoes, where they had hung from plants. The next summer, I became the fire-keeper, which was my favourite job of all. I dunked the basket of tomatoes into the boiling water and pulled it out with a rush of steam after a thirty count; five seconds too long, and the tomatoes would be mushy. Nonna shouted out instructions and praise: "*Brava Anna, fai cossi* – Good Anna, do it like this," and to the others: "*Anna sta fa uno bello lavoro* – Anna is doing a good job!" But their opinions and praise didn't matter – as long as my nonna praised me, I was pleased with myself.

My nonna. I had a nickname for her: Saint Anna, keeper of the tomatoes and everything good to eat.

When we were done canning for the day, the men went inside to the basement where they played cards and drank. They invited my father to join them, just as they did during every gathering, but he always declined. Any other man would have been mocked for staying behind with the women and children, but he was considered a good man. My dad is the one who everyone in the family turned to for help with building cabinets, wiring a house, installing tiles, and he never said an unkind word about any woman. My mother used to say proudly, "I swore I wouldn't marry a drunk like my father or an Italian, and I didn't."

When every vegetable had been boiled, broiled, cut, seasoned, and jarred, summer was over. Cool air stained the leaves yellow, the garden was cut down, the soil turned, and baking season began.

My grandmother's thick muscles under loose, olive skin mesmerized me. Each time she rolled the dough inward, her muscles relaxed, and when she pushed it back out, biceps blossomed. She was covered in sweat that would drip rhythmically into the dough with each addition of water, flour, sugar, and eggs. She laughed from deep within her belly: "I don't need as much salt this way – when I let my sweat fall. *Siamo tutti famiglia* – We're family."

The thought of my grandmother's salty sweat mixed into

the pastry pleased me. It meant I would grow to be strong like her, whether I ate my vegetables or not. She was proud of her strength. My nonna depended upon her body, the same as she depended upon the harvest.

"*Annina*, I hope you use your *testa* more than your *mannine* – use your head more than your hands. *Capische?* Understand? I need to be strong – learn from your *nonna*. Learn everything you can. *Deve essere furba.* You need to be smart."

As she worked the dough, I revelled in the rise and fall of her breasts, waiting for her words, her stories. I felt special. I secretly believed that Nonna loved me more than her other grandchildren. I knew it was wrong to think it, but I was her eldest grandchild and named after her. There is more to a name than consonants and vowels; I knew this. My name was a thread, an anchor to the olive skin covering my bones, and to my family tree.

Nonna knew every twig, weaving them in our kitchen theatre. I listened as though my life depended upon her breath. She punctuated her words with the rise and fall of her hands. Hands tough as hide, palms wide, fingers short and thick. Hands that picked three tomatoes for every one I picked. Factory hands that could set a sleeve in a minute. Hands that sowed seed, milked teats, and brushed my unruly hair. Hands with a story as wide and deep as the ocean she crossed to come here to Canada.

Once she said to me, "Remember this, *Annina*, and it will save you a lot of trouble. Men, *uomi*, are born with golden balls. *Capische?* – Do you understand? *No e tutte rose alla vita,* life is not a bunch of roses. You'll see, my *Annina. . . . Mia mamma, tua bisnonna* – my mother, your great-grandmother, married a handsome man. He left her with *dieci bambini*. Ten babies, and no money. She was too good, Anna. She took care of us. *Povera donna*, poor woman." She pushed the fringe of hair away from her face and made the sign of the cross.

I nodded, but I didn't understand what she meant until much later.

"Now, we need to let the dough rise, *Annina*."

Before she could tell me to go upstairs, I pleaded, "Tell me about when you were a baby."

"Ah, no . . ." she teased, with a tug on my ear, her rough hands soft on my face. "You need sun. You won't grow if you spend all of your time inside with an old woman. Go play. *Fai la brava*, be good."

Leaving her side was like walking out of the sunshine into cold air. I sat at the foot of the giant oak tree across the street, and felt sad. I hoped this meant I had taken some of my grandmother's hurt away. I pictured the break in her heart getting smaller until it was crimson and perfectly shaped like a heart on a Valentine's Day card.

My grandmother used to speak about her body as though it were an island: free-floating, renewable, isolated. Unlike the land she had farmed under a hot sun in Mirabella Eclano, Nonna's body had no seasons; long days and shorter ones, perhaps, but no seasons. Her body was strong, her heart reticent.

I am a red dress

The one story she wouldn't tell me was her own. I tried to understand my nonna, her story, through what she offered – her hands, her eyes, her touch.

Compass

I never called my uncle by his first name. Sometimes *Zio* or *Zi* for short, but mostly Frog. His friends joked that he was so ugly, he looked like a frog (even though none of them had ever seen one). When they threw down wrinkled dollar bills on the backyard paved in concrete, betting on who would fuck Gina first, they called him frog prince and made puckering, lip-smacking sounds. Frog told them to kiss his hairy ass and called them faggots and cocksuckers. They'd talk about Gina's rack and whether or not she puts out. Frog would say, "I had her – she purred real nice like that bike I'm gonna get."

"In your dreams, big man." They'd grunt back in unison, "The only thing you got between your legs is a boner."

"Down to here man, down to here," he bragged, smacking the inside of his thigh. Frog always had a quick comeback. They'd noisily slap each other on the back and throw back their heads laughing till old Signora Rossi, who lived next door, would try to interrupt their fun by singing "Our Father Who Art in Heaven" through her kitchen window.

The first summer I remember them out in my grandmother's backyard, I was five and they were thirteen; it was 1975. The Captain & Tennille were at the top of the charts with "Love Will Keep Us Together" and I thought my uncle Frog and his friends were the coolest. For that entire summer, Signora Rossi implored, *Raggazzi, per piacere* – boys, please. They never bothered to glance at her; they carried on like they hadn't heard a thing. She complained to my grandmother too, but Nonna said they're just being boys and besides, she figured it was better for them to be in the backyard making noise than on the street running around doing who knows what. By the time August rolled around, Signora Rossi was done trying to goad them into being quieter hellions. She would slide open her kitchen window with a loud bang and yell out, *Ziti* or *T'a mazze* – quiet or I'll kill you – over and over again as she caught rivulets of sweat on her embroidered handkerchief. But they didn't pay attention to this either. They were on top of the world, and there was no place to go but higher.

Soon, the leaves turned. When the cold came, they moved their sideshow indoors. They were still noisy, though. Signora Rossi had resolved to come up with a new tactic during the crisp winter months: "Ave Maria," sung in a vibrating soprano with all the zeal she could muster, usually worked like a charm, unless they were drinking beer out of Coke cans, and then they couldn't care less.

They'd toss beer caps across the yard like they were skimming rocks across a lake. I never tossed the caps myself, but I'd watch them from behind the metal bars on the porch. Once, Spoon called over to me, "Hey, did you see that? I kicked Frog's ass." I had a secret crush on Spoon. Sometimes he winked at me when the others weren't looking and said, "You're gonna be a pro at this soon, just like me." He was a bad boy in the grown-up world that I wasn't allowed into, but I knew he was kind underneath all the cussing and fighting; he let me sneak sips from his can, and never said a word to anyone about it.

"Oh yeah, watch this!" Frog hit the top of the wooden fence at just the right angle, and the cap popped up and hit Signora Rossi's window with a clank. She retreated into her house screaming, *Disgrazziate* – bastards! Frog strutted around with his hand up in the air, shouting, "Who's the man?" He and his friends slapped hands with rounds of high fives, low fives, and super-fly handshakes.

No matter how many times the police knocked on the door about busted-up phone booths, parking meters, or pilfered candy bars, my grandmother always considered them to be good boys. And anyone who said anything to the contrary – including priests, teachers, or cops – got a piece of her mind.

There were two things I was sure of at the time: if I got into half as much trouble as they did, I'd spend half my life digging myself out of a giant shit pile, bare-handed; and my uncle wasn't ugly, not even a bit.

When he was just a wriggling newborn, my nonna held him up to the light through the window so she could have a good look at him. She was struck by his beauty. It could be said that every mother thinks her baby is the most beautiful, perfect child. But my nonna was an exception. She thought her first two kids were the ugliest things she'd ever seen. Rai-sin-like wrinkly little things. But not Frog – she was breath-taken; nonetheless, she gave his bum, smaller than the palm of her hand, a good hard smack. Of course, he cried for a long while. She wanted him to know what life was about right away; that it was hard. And besides, there was something about Frog – something different from her other children.

Superstition and magic rule Nonna's world more than religion or reason. I can't say exactly what her magic is – what it looks like, what she does – but I do know that it's rooted in the earth, in the fields she farmed as a child. Rooted in the elements that devastated or raised up crops rich with green. Magic that was whispered between women through villages, surreptitiously carried in small pouches on cow paths under a studded sky. Magic that was diluted upon arriving in Canada, in Toronto, where for all but a couple of weeks in the winter when snowfall slowed traffic to a crawl, the world operated on different principles – ruled by clocks, bus schedules, and science – rather than the body's language, mysteries of the earth, faith in the unseen and unknown.

Nonna saw colours around Frog, mostly violet and a dark shadow. She was so startled by her vision, she nearly dropped him. *La maladetto*, the curse; she saw it in Frog. She had only seen *la maladetto* one other time, in a little girl who died a short while later in her sleep without explanation. She spit into the palm of her hand, rubbed his face gently, pressed him to her breast, and invoked the Virgin Mary and a host of spirits for protection. Behind her back, she pressed her two middle fingers into her palm, with thumb, little finger, and index pointed outward: *le corne* – another invocation to ward off harm.

Destiny, when taunted, when disbelieved, can grow deeper, become more set; it can take a turn for the worse, like the eye of a tornado devastating everything in its path.

Every full moon, she prayed for answers. How could she protect her boy without knowing where the harm would come from? All she heard in response to her pleas was this: *Love your child, love him as best you can. He will be lost in a forest without a compass. Love him so he will find his way home, even when your heart is broken, love him. This is the only principle, the only magic, the only law.*

†

A long time ago, before I was born – before I was even an idea or the heat that swelled in my mother's breasts down, down, down through her body like a falling star in the night – you were running into the wind. This is how I imagine you, Frog, even now when the thought of you running, running anywhere, is difficult to picture. You in your big boots, beer belly bursting against and over your belt, a drink in one hand, a smoke in the other. A forlorn expression on your face, wrinkled and lined beyond your years, nose and brows pulled into an unmistakable *Don't fuck with me* scowl. The gravity of you so heavily pinned to the ground. The weight of your presence cast a shadow, even in your mother's house, especially in your mother's house, where you raged quiet and sure, where you grew to mythic proportions. At the age of fifteen, you were six feet tall and everyone thought that was it; no one in the family is taller than five foot ten, except for Rocco (and he's not blood related). But you grew and grew and didn't stop till you were six-foot-four. A whole head above the rest of us.

I have pictures of you. Snuck them from Mom and Dad's house. Mom said a hundred times over the years, "I'll make a nice album for you." But she never did, and wouldn't let anyone near them – dozens upon dozens of envelopes filled with prints and negatives carefully taped into freezer bags – stashed inside the credenza, the hutch where the alcohol was kept. I tiptoed across the hallway, took what was most precious; a few prints from each envelope, the ones I liked most. I suppose it was my way of trying to keep some of you, or to get to know you. After they took you away, I didn't know if I would see you again, or if I would want to.

One day, our family came apart like an old, thread-bare sheet. Nonna had gone to church as she did every Sunday morning. Mom and Dad and I went over to Nonna's house for lunch, and Zio Giuseppe and Zia Rachaela dropped by later with coffee cake. It wasn't particularly unusual that you and Lucy and the boys weren't there, and to be honest, I was relieved – not that Lucy, Sam, and Peter weren't there – but that you weren't. My stomach turned every time you yelled at the boys and picked at Lucy about what a fat slob she was. You'd pace around the kitchen table, down the hallway to

33

the front door, and back through the kitchen. Without fail, Nonna set a plate for you even though you never ate anything. She'd pat the chair next to her and plead, "Come sit. I made the chicken nice – just the way you like it."

Mom said the things the rest of us were thinking, but never said. "Look at you, Frog – you got the shakes and you can't wait to pour your next drink."

"Mind your own fuckin' business."

"Well, stop making it my business. Why don't you go to a bar instead of coming to Mom's house. Oh right, I forgot – the booze is free here."

And then you'd screech out of the driveway. Nonna would sit there wringing her hands, glass-eyed, muttering to herself or to God. She would not, could not, be consoled by us. The only tenderness she accepted was from her cat Chico, purring, swishing, and circling around her ankles until she reached down to stroke his ginger coat. We'd cover the leftovers with wax paper, wash the dishes, say our good-byes with kisses on both cheeks, and drive Lucy and the boys home in silence. We knew there would be hell to pay, but we weren't the ones you'd be going home to.

All those years Nonna had been praying to keep you safe, fearing that you would be hurt. She couldn't see that someone else's blood would spill, that you would be the one left standing.

Time stopped that day and became a compass, a road to every place thereafter, a cool north wind, dawn from the east, fire from the south, twilight from the west. We did not grow stronger like the cliché about tragedy bringing family closer together. We scattered like beads from a stretched necklace. One went this way, the other that. We continued to have lunch together on Sundays with Italian voices on the radio humming in the background, and exchanged words about the weather, the specials at Kmart, anything but you. Nonna continued to set a plate for you as though you'd stop in any minute, and even Mom knew not to say anything about it.

You were a child once. It would be easy to forget this in light of who you are today. The smiling little prankster, always working on a fool-proof scheme, building bigger and stronger fortresses, is all but gone. Where did you recede to? You were a boy once. Curls raging against the rare summer breeze. A smile that sailed me into the next day that came, and came.

Promise

My nonna had rabbits, but they were as good as mine. She lived right across the street from us, on the other side of Dufferin Street, and I visited them every day during the summer. One Sunday after I shoveled back my lunch, I set my empty plate on the kitchen counter, and ran into the backyard to pet the rabbits. Nonna called to me from the table, "Anna, come eat some more *coniglio*!" I heard her but didn't say a word; all I could do was look at the rabbits' small, blinking eyes, all dark and shiny like a bowl of Glossettes. She had said come eat some more rabbit. My knees buckled, and I hit the concrete hard.

My mother came out to the back yard. "What's wrong, Anna?" she asked, caressing my cheek. "Come on, don't upset your Nonna . . . stand up."

"You lied," I sputtered. I was being dramatic, but couldn't help it. "You said we were eating chicken. *Nonnina* just said *coniglio*. I heard her. She, she, she said . . ." I sobbed, snot dripping down my face onto my green and white striped polyester ⊤-shirt.

"Okay, Anna, okay. Can't we have just one Sunday without a scene? *Basta* – enough! Stand up now." Pink blush rose at her neck, framed by her black hair and the plunging neckline of her flower-print dress.

My mother's words sunk in. A scene? It was a warm, sunny day. The only kind I remember well. Next door, Signora Rossi's *nipotine*, her many grandchildren, were playing hide-and-seek behind the grapevines that covered a big arbor-like structure made of old pipes that had been welded together. They sounded like fire engines. *Whrrr whrrr weeeee*, over and over again. God, that's so stupid, I thought. You're gonna be found in three seconds flat. If I can see you from behind the fence, so can anyone. But they were only little and I was six, almost a grown-up. If I hadn't been in the middle of a crisis, I would have shown them how to play the game right, how to use time-outs and how to throw stones so the seeker thinks you're where the sound is, and not where you really are.

Signora Rossi's teenaged grandsons, who parked their Mustang in the middle of my nonna's shared driveway, were arm-wrestling on the picnic table they had ripped off from Earlscourt Park. I knew they stole it because the engraved metal nameplate was still on it. Vito won, as usual. I don't know why Tony kept arm-wrestling with him. He'd already lost all his gold series hockey cards and *Playboy* magazines on their bets. I'd seen Tony pull one of those magazines out from under his T-shirt and hand it over grudgingly. They hid them in the garage where I hid during hide-and-seek once, so I knew what was in them.

None of them were paying any attention to me. It was

just another Sunday. But I thought they should have been looking, at least. They were probably all rabbit killers too. Why would they care that I didn't believe in Santa Claus or the Easter Bunny, but that I did believe everything my grandmother said? I loved those rabbits.

Nonna came out of the house with my brother Johnny. My mother whispered something into Nonna's ear. Johnny stood behind her, wearing a T-shirt that matched mine, his tongue sticking out at me and his button nose scrunched up like a ball of yarn. I would have kicked him, but I couldn't move my legs.

"*Annina*. . . ." When my grandmother called me *Annina* I felt special. Except for now. I just felt sick to my stomach. I had counted the rabbits and two of them were missing. My grandmother cooed, "You didn't understand your nonna. We're eating chicken." I didn't respond. She turned to my mother, "When are you going to teach her Italian?"

Whenever they talked about something interesting, or something they thought I shouldn't hear, they'd tell me I didn't understand what they were saying. I played along most times because all the best stories were told in Italian. Not this time. I wasn't going to play pretend.

"You're lying. I heard you!" I screamed through gasps. I couldn't see my nonna, my mom, or Johnny because of the tears pouring out of my eyes.

My grandmother threw up her hand. "*Dio mio* – my God, see – I told you not to let her play with them! Now she thinks they're pets." She turned toward me. "*Annina*, there's nothing wrong with eating *coniglio*. We eat it in Italy all the time."

I sulked, "I hate Italy."

My grandmother's face went white as a sheet of snow, and my tears stopped running. I had crossed the line, and my grandmother crossed herself – *nome de Padre, Figlio, Spirito Santo* – in the name of the Father, Son, Holy Spirit – and then went back inside the house without saying another word. I didn't really know what I was saying, but I knew enough to not have said it. My grandmother spoke about Italy like it was a long lost lover. I had hurt her. I didn't know where Italy was, or why it mattered so much. I just hoped she would let me brush her long hair again and tell me stories.

Satisfied that the drama was over, my mother went back inside with my brother following behind. The rabbits blinked back at me through wire mesh. I wanted to promise them that nothing bad would happen, but I didn't. Promises are meant to be kept.

Blow

She calls me darling. Darling you, to be exact. I see fine china, petticoats, ankles screaming for breeze. Somewhere I've never been. She remakes the word, profane and delicate. Balanced against her landscape, her lips are snapdragons in bloom. I am wind-blown wheat, bending to her pause. My shoulders drop. A sigh (hers or mine?) fills the room. Even snapdragons need rest, all this talk is tiresome. She splits me open in a breath. There is a place on her body between steel eyes and swell of breasts. That place, that perfect place, I am seeing for the first time. Her collarbone a cup, full flowing over. I imagine her breath curled there under skin, bone, muscle – ready to leap forward, like a snake, rise up, fill me.

I am a red dress

Two.

I remember being a girl, eyes like stars falling, big hair bun-
dled like celery. Young Catholic girl, standing at the altar,
the precipice. Quiet Maltese-Italian girl, walking the long
stretch of a moment. Perfectly still angel, open-mouthed
bride. Two seconds passed, maybe three.

    The priest whispered *Body and blood of Christ.* His eyes
mournful, cavernous. Arm outstretched like a spoke, the wa-
fer wheel dangling. I did not scratch my bum, but I thought
about it, about our terrible dresses. About his ominous
gown, my scratchy polyester. About the nauseated swell that
danced in my stomach at the sight, the smell, of meat. How
I pushed it to the edge of my plate, banished it from my uni-
verse. But it did not go away. I had to eat it, it cost money:
blood, sweat, tears, years, youth. *This is bread,* I told myself.
This is bread – not blood, not body, not Jesus. Inhale, hold it,
pretend I'm underwater. Close my eyes, swallow, count.

THREE.

I held my breath and counted for twenty years. Waited patiently for the other shoe to drop, only half believing it ever would. Waited for a window to open, for my throat to loosen, for fresh air, a change of air, a disaster, a miracle. All of this happened. A symphony of chaos, the harmonics of a life spilled over, uncorked.

I am a red dress

FOUR.

Wind-blown ankles scream for breeze. This perfect place,
the long stretch of this moment. Walking between steel eyes
and swell of breasts, her lips are snapdragons in bloom. She
remakes language, profane, and delicate. Two seconds pass,
maybe three. Her breath curls there, dances in my stomach.
A symphony of chaos. She calls me darling, in a breath, I
fall open.

Salt Water

I show up on her doorstep a few times a year with badly wrapped, nearly wilted carnations from the corner store. My chin rests on her crown of wispy hair during our brief embrace. She kisses my cheeks and cries; I taste salt hot on my tongue. I'm sure that my nonna thinks it's the last time she'll see me; it's like that with us. I visit sporadically, and am careful to be noncommittal about my next visit. I don't want to mislead her – and I am equally concerned not to box myself into a promise that I won't keep.

She sweeps my hair away from my face, and braces my shoulders as if to steady me. She takes my soft hands in her leathery ones and spreads my palms flat, as though they are a map. I wonder if she sees anything – if she's looking for something in particular – but I don't ask. I wrest my hands free; the intimacy of the gesture is overwhelming. I shove them awkwardly into the pockets of my jeans. Silence falls between us, and is swiftly carried away by a current of activity.

I unwrap the flowers and cut the end off each stalk on a sharp diagonal. At the kitchen sink, Nonna turns the tap on until cold water gushes out at full force. I fill a mason jar with water and a spoonful of sugar, arrange the flowers, and place them on the kitchen table. They're a sad-looking bunch, but their vibrant pink brings brightness to the beige room. She opens the fridge and pulls out cheese, yesterday's chicken, and green beans dressed in olive oil and garlic. I offer to help, but she shoos me from the counter. "*Siedi, Annee* – sit down, Anna."

I rub the clear plastic that covers the embroidered tablecloth. My nonna looks smaller than when I last watched her press a knife into a cheese round. The kitchen looks precisely as it did when I was a child – preserved as my memories. A print of Jesus and the twelve disciples eating the Last Supper is on the wall across from the table. A wooden cross hangs above the door that leads into the hallway. The photo of my great-grandmother, in a plastic gold frame, sits in the credenza, where the good plates and crystal bowls are kept.

My grandmother fills the espresso pot and turns the tap back down. She wrings her hands as if they are wet laundry and wipes them on the front of her black dress. She has been wearing black since my grandfather Ernesto died, but before then too. All of her clothes – skirts, dresses, pants, sweaters – have been signalling a constant mourning for as long as I can remember.

I pull a paper napkin from the holder and fold it into a makeshift plane – I am eight years old all over again, with scabby knees and braids down to my bum. I close one eye and mark my flight path through the doorway. Just as I'm about to release the plane, sure that this one will make it all the way to the front door, my uncle Mike shuffles in with a tumbler in hand. "Well, look at what the wind blew in."

45

I stand to hug him. He smells like rolled tobacco and soap. "You look like hell," I say. I like Mike, always have. I count on him for good banter. The rest of the family stopped bringing up politics around me years earlier, but Mike enjoys a debate. We seldom agree on anything, except to agree to disagree, but we laugh a lot with one another and sometimes at ourselves.

He ruffles my hair. "So, you dropped in to fly planes or to spread some good cheer?"

"Why don't you go put on a shirt or something, Mike?"

"Nice to see you too." A wide smirk calls attention to his high cheekbones – the envy of the women in our family. He fills his glass, holds the bottle out at me.

"Thanks, but I'll pass. I need my wits about me."

"Oh yeah – well I don't. I'll put one back for you." He raises his glass to me and returns to the television. The volume is so high that the TV may as well be on the kitchen table. The Leafs are down 2 to 1 against the Calgary Flames, and it's late in the third period. Things aren't looking good for the home team, but it doesn't much matter to me who wins.

The espresso pot sounds a rolling gurgle. "*Nonnee*, I'll fix you a cup. *Tu voi lo zucchero* – do you want sugar?"

"*No, grazie*, Anna." She sets the food down with some bread and a small bowl of olive oil and balsamic vinegar and, finally, settles herself into a chair with a sigh.

I place two cups of espresso on the table, both black, and lean in to give her a peck. She turns to offer me the side of her face without the birthmark. I plant a kiss and ask, "How are you – *come stai, Nonnee?*" as I brush the wayward hairs from her face.

She fusses with a bobby pin, the loose skin on her upper arms swaying like a sheet hung out to dry. "I have nothing left . . . I used to have a nice head of hair, like you – *come te.*"

"You're still beautiful *Nonnee*, just older."

"*Ragazzina* – young girl, you're the only one who tells me I'm beautiful anymore." She smiles, and it's clear where Mike's high cheekbones came from.

"That means you should listen to me, Nonna." I briefly touch her forearm, dotted with brown spots, before scooping beans onto my plate.

Mike calls out from the living room, "Hey Anna, will you bring me the bottle – the JD?"

"What's wrong with your legs, Mike? Get up off your lumpy ass and come sit with us a while."

My grandmother grimaces and leans her weight into the table to rise from the chair. I motion to her. "Sit down, *Nonnee*, I'll get it."

Mike winks at me as I drop the bottle into his lap. "Yeah, you're welcome, you lazy ass," I say.

"Hey, I'm just relaxing, but there's plenty for you to do around here – I got a jacket over there missing a couple buttons."

"Yeah, sure – why don't I throw a load in while I'm at it. I'll be sure to separate your silk boxers from your briefs."

"Hey – you're still the kid around here. Doesn't matter

47

if you're thirty. You should call me Uncle Mike – Mr Uncle Mike."

"Don't hold your breath, Mike." We laugh in unison.

In the kitchen, my grandmother is buzzing around the sink. "*Nonnee*, come sit."

She settles again, and that same tentative silence rises between us like a monolith. Our relationship is a poetry of disconnection and reconnection – of blood stories, nostalgia, and trying to make meaning of the senseless.

My grandmother imbues everything with meaning. If a full glass falls, it has nothing to do with a cluttered table – it's a sign from God about the harvest going bad, or a cheque bouncing, or good health. She doesn't believe in random events.

I was born on a night when the moon was full, as was my grandmother. According to my nonna, and to her mother, the sky was so bright with light, not one star could be seen. It follows that both our births, on nights when the moon was full and no stars shone, is not coincidental. She used to say that we are either cursed or blessed – bound together by our names, and the moon.

Over ten years ago, my grandmother and I became tied by a moment that changed everything between us. The once level ground that we stood on shifted irrevocably, and now, the place where we meet slopes sharply; I step carefully, wary not to slide.

I had been visiting my nonna as I had done most Sundays for all of my life. Our visits had become increasingly important to me since my late teens – I was aware of her poor health, and she had more time to visit with me, which I took great pleasure in. When I was a child, moments alone with my grandmother were precious and rare, something always called her away: a pot that needed stirring, clothes that needed ironing, or one of the neighbours at the door for a cup of flour.

There had been no special occasion for our visit that day. We ate lunch together, and afterward I watered the vegetable garden in the back yard. My grandmother seemed agitated, but she was often busy with worry about our family or the bills that needed to be paid, and she was also on a new medication that made her jumpy. She placed her hand on top of mine, signalling me to turn off the water.

"What's wrong, Nonna?"

She rubbed her eyes and took a deep breath. "I've been dreaming about the Virgin Mary every night since winter time." Many of my grandmother's stories began and ended with the Virgin Mary, but there was an urgency in her then that I hadn't sensed before.

"*Nell miei sogni* – in my dreams, the Sorrowful Virgin – *L' Adolorata* – spread her arms. *Suo cuore* – her heart – *brilla con la luce* – shone with a bright light, and her eyes rained down a river of tears. In the last dream, *L' Adolorata ca veva uno bello soriso ma uno sguardo severo* – the Virgin had a loving but stern expression. *Lei m' adetto devo justare tutte le cose in ordine* – she told me that it was time to set my house in order – that I must set things right."

49

My grandmother began to cry and shake. I put my arms around her, but she pulled away and told me to listen to her until she was done. This is the story she told me:

She was climbing down the basement stairs to retrieve a jar of tomatoes. She heard a strange sound, so she quieted her step and stopped climbing about halfway down, then peered the rest of the way. She saw my grandfather's hands on my shoulders, pressing my body down onto his penis. In the shock of the moment, she didn't know what to do. She made the sign of the cross – nome de Padre, Figlio, Spirito Santo *– and prayed that what she had witnessed would never happen again. She turned away, and walked back up the stairs.*

I lost vision for an instant, my throat tightened, and tears ran down my face while I struggled for air. My grandmother stepped toward me. I jumped back and hit the doorframe. I pressed my weight into it to steady myself.

"How old was I?" I asked.

She hesitated, but only briefly. "*Cinque* – five."

I slid down the doorframe with my hands pressed to my ears. Pressure gathered and popped as if I was on a plane on a rapid descent path. I was flooded with pictures of Nonna and I – of me following her around like a wet-nosed puppy – of the six horrible years that had followed the day my grandmother walked away.

I wheezed, "Why, Nonna? Why are you telling me this?" But I ran out of her house without waiting for her answer. I didn't know where to go; my sense of home turned on its

head. The thought of getting on a bus with strangers was unbearable, so I walked and ran intermittently. Eventually, my
legs took me home to the tiny house on Plymouth Avenue
that my friend Gwen and I rented. When Gwen arrived, she
found me huddled on the living room floor, and held me for
a long time while I cried and rocked my body back and forth
like a see-saw.

Feelings of betrayal and loss far outweighed any anger I
felt for my grandmother. I turned the story over a hundred
times and no matter how I approached it, I couldn't make
sense of it. How had she lived with that knowledge – the
reality of what she saw, and then the memory of it, without
doing anything?

She became two distinct people for me on the day she
told her horrible story: my beloved childhood Nonna on
whom I doted, and my grandmother who abandoned me. I
spend time with her, and I am begrudgingly aware that she is
both Nonna and grandmother – a woman who caressed me
with her right hand and pushed me away with her left.

A couple of months later, I travelled to the other end of
Canada. I didn't see my grandmother again for another five
years, when I was twenty-seven – but I thought of her often.

"*Annee?* Anna?" The sound of Nonna's voice pulls me
back into the room, into present day.

"Yeah, *Nonnee.*"

"Mangia, Anna – eat. *Tu bisogno la forza* – you need your
strength."

I reach for a piece of bread and she returns to the sink. I watch her move, but I don't entirely recognize the woman I see there. I miss her – the woman she was, to the child I was then. I see glimpses of it, but mostly I imagine her walking away from me. It's as though she taught me to be strong so that I could survive being left behind.

My grandmother and I are the poetry of disconnection and reconnection – of blood stories, memory, and trying to make meaning of the senseless. The place where we meet slopes sharply; I am wary not to slide.

I have forgiven my grandmother, but I haven't forgotten anything.

House of Cards

i. Shuffle

My grandfather's lungs collapsed like a house of cards, and the rest of his body followed. A ship at sea without sails. Was it two decks a day, home-brew, or hate that caused his capsize? This story, the body only tells part of.

II. CUT

Had he been cut open, the doctors would have found cancer like wild bluebells. Multiple and hybrid, a miracle of fecundity. Biblical seed between rocks: inflamed vital organs, distended stomach, cirrhotic liver crystalline green, coagulated blood dark as tar. A body in a state of disaster. A site of emergency, of emergence. What does hate do to a body, to a self?

III. DEAL

This story is the pink of recent incision. A scar that stretches across abdomen, ocean, time. This story is old, long forgotten. (Better) remembered here. Told by the daughter of a daughter of a father. This story is clip/skid. A collision of perspectives, generations, metaphor. This story twists and creaks like a broken bow. Recorded here, is a/new vision.

iv. Hand

Billboards appear along the Don Valley Parkway: Welcome to Toronto: City of Love and Buried Rivers, Warning: Hate is a Scalpel, Handle with Care. Under highways and streets that loop through the city like macramé, lost rivers flow: Mud Creek, Garrison Creek, Taddle Creek. If you press your ear to the ground and remain very still, you can hear them. They offer a world of possibility, our very own Atlantis. Any attempts to excavate must be done with great care.

I am a red dress

v. FLUSH

Between my grandfather and me, there is a legacy of hate
and with it, a strange, suspect creature. A legacy of love.
Tell me you love me, he whispered, *Tell me you love me.* This
is love? This gnarled thing he pressed into me, this sour-
ness here in the dark, this is love? Consonants, vowels, alphabet soup, tumbled down from the kitchen upstairs where
my family broke bread. Before love, I knew its absence. This
hollow, is this love?

VI. Solitaire

Opposites do not attract, they shine a light on one another: reflectors on a northern freeway, shorn wheat crop circles in the middle of the prairie, in the middle of God's country where there is no end of sky. In the name of love we fall down. We hurt one another. We are felled like old-growth trees. We count our rings, lose centre, lose count, lose story. In the name of love, we are revisionist historians creating a past that is easier to live by. But roots remain, like buried rivers. Here is a count, an account, a rhythm; a story emerges from what remains.

I am a red dress

VII. Fold

It's a wonder any one of us in my family manages to put one
foot in front of the other. Shame that came with birth grew
deeper each sunrise. I was no exception. Years of practice;
pretending I was alright when I was torn up and tired. Lived
like I wasn't worth a cent. Took chances I didn't have, my
head a mess. Alphabet soup.

VIII. TRUMP

I broke the only rule that bound my family together: started with don't, ended with can't. I did speak.

I am a red dress

ix. Stakes

One year after I filed sexual assault charges against my grandfather, he was sentenced to a three-year term in a federal
penitentiary. Released after two, special dispensation was
given to him for being an inky old man, a model prisoner. He
pled wrong-doing to the right people. I was not among them.
Judicial is a peculiar word. How can justice be dispensed for
something so irreconcilable? A rolling back of time?

Anna Camilleri

x. Poker Face

My grandmother told anyone who asked that my grandfather had returned to Italy to rest – that he, who had never before been on holiday, was spending two years vacationing in his homeland. When he returned from his trip, she welcomed him back into the house as though nothing had changed – as though nothing had happened to begin with.

·

xi. Joker

Before he started howling my name in his last days, before
he wept like a baby left out on a stoop, before his fear of
death – its inevitability, its closeness – before his righteous-
ness waned, there was no contrition from his lips. Instead,
the belief strong and sure, that he had taken what was his to
take. If a man is not the king of his own castle, he is nothing.
Flesh of my flesh. Blood of my blood. Body of my body.

XII. TRICK

Prior to his death, prayer became his refuge. He confused me
with the Virgin Mary, exchanging our names glibly like two
short-handled umbrellas – one easily mistaken for the other.
Hail child full of grace. Fruit of thy womb. Mother here on earth.
You are blessed amongst women and girls. In my grandfather's
re-creation, I became divine and untouched, and he, a mis-
directed penitent.

XIII. FULL HOUSE

Contrary to other family events that had come and gone
– macabre baptisms with even more macabre hymns, over-
done weddings, bridal showers with strange ribbon bonnet
rituals – to which I was not invited, or conditionally invited,
my presence was not disputed at my grandfather's funeral.
There was not even a suggestion, on this day, of what would
be appropriate for me to wear. This would be the day when
I could be as I wished, unfettered. This would have been the
day to rage about all that had gone wrong, to shout about
what a lousy excuse for a family this convergence of people
was; some familiar, familial, others a sliver of memory from
another time. This didn't happen. I did not rage. I wanted
my rage back – white knuckled, hungry, alive. Slip/skid.

xiv. In Spades

The day of the funeral of my dead grandfather, the chapel is filled with black coats, black dresses, black shoes shined just for the day. We look our most solemn best. White tissues float and bob like foam after cresting waves. In the air is the acrid/ sickeningly sweet smell that only funeral parlours have. It's time to mourn now. Shed a penny or two to help him pass on. Give the boat a good solid kick so it doesn't come back the same way. Hold a rosary, say a prayer. Take stock, try not to feel. Here, crying is sanctioned. But the tears are bitter.

There is a thin veneer in this theatre of loss and missing and love. There is anger and hate and hurt.

I am a red dress

xv. SUIT

My grandfather is wearing a freshly pressed navy blue suit, his hands joined by a rosary. He is a small man. His rouged cheeks are sunken, but he looks healthier than he has in years. I kneel at the casket, and I am only a little afraid that his eyes will open. I expect to feel anger or joy, but neither is present. I am sad – for my grandfather, for myself, for all of us. I wish him a better journey the next time around. I rise and turn to my family, and silently wish each one love, knowing that never again will any of us love with the brave heart of a child; but we will love, each in our own way. My mother and my grandmother take me by the hand and wrap me with their bodies. Something new takes root. A stretch of road, a circle to stand in, a centre.

XVI. QUEEN OF HEARTS

The wreckage of my grandfather's life spreads out on the sea floor. Underwater, we are the beautiful splinters, smooth rocks, torn masts, broken bow. We are a collection of nearly got away, got away, a mix of fresh off the boat pull yourself out of the shit mythology, first and now second generation dealing with the shit of the mythology, illiterates, jailbirds, workers, depressives, makin' good in a suit careful not to lean to heavy on the GS like Italians do, brittle with arthritic bones, DTS, wrinkles, and still soft baby skin. We are synchronized swimmers, out of practice at moving in unison. We fan, move, suck, like blind single cell amoebae. Each in our own moment.

Family portrait: There's my uncle Mike wearing a crisp white shirt and black slacks, straining to reach for his mickey. My brother's hands are shoved deep into his pockets. My father, by the door, is wearing a stricken expression unknown to me. My grandmother is wailing and cursing for all that cannot be undone. My mother has never looked so sad, never stood so tall. She is not wearing a red dress.

Mother

Mother, one stone is wedged across the hole in

our history

and sealed with blood wax.

In this hole is our side of the story . . .

It is the half that has never been told,

and some of us must tell it.

— LORNA GOODISON

Lexicon of the Red Dress, part 2

If my mother could have willed my grandfather dead, believe me, he would have been gone long before his passing. She had many reasons to despise my grandfather. We all did – each of us with our own slow-shifting stories, overlapping like colossal tectonic plates.

I assumed that my mother's venom for my grandfather was related to the unkind and often brutal ways he treated my grandmother Anna, the frequent beatings my mother endured at his hands, the way he drank away my grandmother's wages.

Still life: Toronto, 1975. This picture has sound. My nonna is holding a bowl with broccoli dressed in olive oil. She's about to put it on the table. My grandfather isn't in the picture, he's in the basement. Before he left the kitchen, he dished food onto his plate and as he passed Nonna he said, "You're nothing to look at – I wouldn't pay ten cents to put my dick in you." I'm sitting next to my father, and my brother Johnny, who just stopped wearing diapers, is on my lap. He looks like a doll; long lashes fan his almond-shaped eyes. My mom is on the other side of me. There's no food on Mom's plate; she's on a diet.

Around the neighbourhood, my grandfather was altogether different; regarded as an affable, charismatic man, ready to empty his pockets for friends in need at a moment's notice. My mother burned with this knowledge: that he was gracious to strangers and cruel to her, that he had ever been born, and that she was born his daughter, his first child.

My mother doesn't believe in life-after-death justice. She doesn't believe in justice at all if it means turning the other cheek, shutting up and putting up.

I remember when Bonnie, the new kid in my grade six class, called me a *wop*. I was sure that that word didn't belong in her mouth, and it didn't belong to me either. The fact that she was dumb enough to call me a *wop* was reason enough for me to smack her. Sweaty kids gathered around and yelled, "Fight! Fight!" the yard abuzz with adrenalin. During our scrap, Bonnie took a clump of my hair along with the elastic band, but I split her lip. I went home with a note from the office that spelled out my punishment for bullying. My mother yelled at me first and asked questions later. When I recounted the story, my mom nodded and said, "She'll think twice before she uses that word again. Don't let anyone walk on you, it's a hard habit to break." And that was the end of it.

For all of my mother's toughness and defiance, I never saw her stand up to my grandfather, but as soon as he left the room she yelled out, "When that bastard dies, I'm going to the funeral in a red dress." Afterward, she looked sad, melancholic.

I am a red dress

I saw rare glimpses of my mother when she was happy, when she took her pleasure in the things her life afforded her: an AM/FM radio, and a body that moved.

The radio was on when my mother was home, without exception. I remember her clipping chunky rollers into her hair while she sang along with Mama Cass, or shuffled to the Pointer Sisters. One night my father grimaced in jest. "It looks like you're building a nest," he said.

She puckered up her lips into a kiss and said, "It's not like we got married and I turned into an old Italian lady. I still go with the fashion." Then she suggestively swung her hips his way. "Oh come on, let's do the hustle."

But my father only smiled and left the room. He is reluctant about displays of affection. Instead, my mom took me by the hands. "Come on, Anna, dance with your mom!" I basked in her attention – in the moments when she shined her eyes on me, which happened less often with every passing year. As a teenager, I was impatient with my mother, but mostly I wanted her to notice me.

"If I could start over again, everything would be different," she mused.

"What would be different, Mom?"

"The lottery would do it. I'd be gone so fast, you'd think I was lightning."

"Yeah, Mom, and what are the chances of that?"

"Jesus, you're so serious, Anna. You've always been so serious."

"Well, it is serious. What would you do differently? If

you could change one thing, what would it be?"

She looked down at her hands. "I'd be a hairdresser," she said tentatively. "I've always wanted to do hair. Maybe I'd open a little shop."

"Mom, you could do that! You'd be great at it."

"Oh, please."

"No, really, you can do it. There's lots of hairdressing schools in Toronto."

"I've never had a head for school, you know that. I don't have a head for much of anything anymore . . . anyway, when your grandfather dies, that'll be my lottery."

"And then what?"

"I'll start over."

The following week, I went home with a stack of books and magazines from the public library. I knew every hairdressing school in the city, every college that offered part-time courses, and how to get a student loan. The number of times I said to her, "You can't change the past, but you can change the future," must have frustrated her to no end. I wanted to rescue my mother, same as I wanted her to rescue me from an unimaginable future.

Cut From the Same Stone

I. JEWEL

My mother was too big for me to hold, even with my entire body wrapped around her tight as could be. She was bigger than life itself. A planet in motion.

I heard her coming before I saw her, shoes clicking up the stairs, then down. When she wasn't dressed for the assembly line, she wore mid-thigh skirts, tops that stopped (or started) at her midriff, mary-jane platforms, deep oval necklines, dark lipstick. I remember one cap-sleeved baby-T in particular. Sky blue with curly silver-sparkle letters printed across her breasts: *Classy Lady*. She created anthems out of swear words, strung together like raging, pink pearls. She would say, "There's no point in being subtle." And she wasn't, about anything.

II. MOTHER OF PEARL

I am quickly approaching mid-life like a meteor gathering speed on its descent; my childhood is a mirage wavering behind me. But I will always be my mother's daughter, her first-born child. She reminds me of this: "The older you get, the more you look like me."

My father scoops more vegetable casserole onto his plate, and winks at me with a smile.

My mom continues, "You'll always look more like your dad, but you're starting to get my ass – you better watch it, Anna, or you'll need bigger chairs."

She is always the first to point out my weight gain or loss. I clear her plate and my own. "Should I put on some tea for us?"

My father responds, "Yeah, *Annee*, but less sugar for me. You made it too sweet last time."

"Less sugar for me too, Anna."

"You take it with one spoon, right?"

"No, half a spoon. We cut back – you know your nanna had diabetes." A few years earlier, I had visited Malta and returned home with news of the doctor's estimate that Nanna had only a few years left. My gut feeling was that she would die sooner, and I had told my father to go to Malta right away; he called home and his brother assured him that Nanna was fine. She died two months later. My father clenches his jaw at the mention of his mother whom he describes as a saint.

My mom brushes his arm. "Anyway, Anna, it doesn't matter if you get big. We all get big – it runs in the family. You'll always be my beautiful girl."

I set down the tea and change the subject. "Did you like the casserole?"

I am a red dress

III. CASTING

When I was a child, my mom and I went to the Toronto
Dominion Bank at the corner of St Clair and Dufferin every
Saturday morning. I waited for her in one of the tan vinyl
chairs that lined the bank's west wall, Dufferin Street rush-
ing past on the other side of the red brick, my feet swinging
inches from the ground. This Saturday, she waved me to join
her at the counter. Franca, the teller who always smelled like
cut flowers, smiled down at me. They talked about work and
their swollen ankles, while I carefully printed my name on
some papers. I was given a little green book – my first chequ-
ing account – with $5.00 printed across the top of the first
page in the deposit column. Mom said, "This is to get you
started. You'll need to earn the rest."

That day, my mother told me that I should never make
the mistake of believing that anyone would take care of me,
and that even if I were to get married, I should have my
own money. She told me I was smart, that I should stay in
school for as long as possible, and I should arm myself with
knowledge, an arsenal of words and ideas. This knowledge
would free me from being leashed like a bitch in waiting, to
a person, a place, to a self sewn together and struggling to
stay as one.

IV. STONE SOUP

My mother was never one to mince words. She was, is, the
cutter, slicing through the divide between what is thought

79

and what is said, between propriety and precision, between what is and what is not. To her, time was always being wasted, and goddamnit, she had no time for that. Two babies before the age of nineteen, a time clock to punch in and out of, laundry waiting to be wrung, a tired husband, a bleeding-heart for a mother, lost brothers, a bastard for a father – and not a soft pair of hands between them. Oh no, she would not raise weak children.

v. Stone's Throw

At the bank that morning, I understood my mother's words as a tale in self-sufficiency, aware of my dependence as a child. Some ten years later, I thought of that day as my first lesson in feminism (even though she never described herself as a feminist). Today, more than twice the age of my mother when she was pregnant with me, I understand my mother's words to be the telling of her story. An inversion, shrouded in double negatives.

In the language of don't, shouldn't, never, not, shouldn't have, won't, abstain, protect, guard, carry, bury, hide, dominate, scavenge, scurry, hurry, hurry, hurry, a story is told – a woman's story, my mother's story, a femme's story. A working-class story about economy of the heart. A story that does not speak the language of I.

A woman became she, we, they. A woman for whom the first

person singular is too bare. A woman cloaked in rich fabric, lined eyes, ample curves, quick tongue, with a heart that cannot afford to bear it's own weight.

I have asked myself, am I the daughter in shadow – eclipsed by my mother's path? A double-negative squared? Will it be her constellation or mine that determines the orbit of this story? Do these questions even make sense? Is it possible to separate a child's story from her mother's?

No clear beginning or end between us – my mother is the alpha and the omega, and I am what lies between.

VI. MILESTONE

1977 is printed vertically along the white border of the photograph. A birthday cake with seven candles and *Happy Birthday* printed in round, red letters in the centre of the frame, and all of us around it – peripheral. Giovanna, Rosaria, Antonia, on one side of the table, elbows perched on rose-print tablecloth. Carina, Kelly, Maria on the other side. Rosaria is my best friend. She lets me bite pieces off her candy necklace. I'm jealous of Maria because she's so pretty, and she just came that way. I don't trust Antonia because she cheats me out at hide 'n' seek every time, but she's my next-door neighbour so she's in all the birthday pictures. I wish I had straight hair like Kelly's, like the girls on TV. Then there is my mother. I'm sitting next to her at the head of the table. I want to cut the cake. The Tre Mare Bakery cake is the best part of my birthday. My mother won't let me cut it until I pose with it for at least six photos. In them, I appear to be underwater; a streak of sunlight mottles my face. My eyes are red and shiny, tears held by lashes. My mother, on the other side of the sun, is dressed in shadow. She is pinching the soft skin under my arm. But this isn't in the picture. She twists tighter, whispers, *Smile*. Photographs don't come with sound. Some meteors do. Fireballs, exceptionally bright meteors, hiss and crackle as they enter our atmosphere.

VII. STICKS AND STONES

Snapshots divide my life like a split river. Somewhere in that year, 1977, maybe that day, I stopped crying. And every photograph thereafter tells the same story.

The drink of choice is Brio Chinotto, homemade red wine, or Molson Ex. *Little girl grows up fast and hates because people are a bunch of thieving liars.* Favourite foods include bread (Calabrese), cheese (asiago), red peppers (roasted), prosciutto (hot), melanzane (in oil), pasta (with sauce). *Little girl is tough as nails, stronger than they think.* The curtains are always drawn. *Little girl does not cry, no matter what.* Fans move hot air in circles; our faces shine with sweat. *Just try to break her.*

VIII. MEDUSA

So much attention is paid to Her body, no one notices she has fallen, and she may not notice this herself. She knows what earth tastes like.

You'll hear about your infractions, your sins against Her. Her displeasure will come in shards.
But the pointed words she speaks are only part of the story.

She returns to the confines of Her body. This circle dance is dizzying. Her body is no stranger to injury and has proven to be strong beyond any reasonable expectation, but this is not the heart of the matter.

She is accustomed to the pedestal she sits upon. The sharpness of the wood, the weight of her ass on it, the distance from the ground. She tells herself it is plush as a throne, but it is little more than a chamber.

The world has left her cold. Her lovers have left her cold. She is cold as a stone.

How do you kiss Medusa? Eyes open or eyes closed?

IX. SKIPPING STONES

For the longest time, I was concerned about being too soft – a soft touch, soft-hearted, soft-spoken. It wasn't until I was about twenty-four that I realized I had buried that part of me long, long ago. I had grown up into an impenetrable woman, an utterly untouchable femme, just like my mother. I had become a girl, then a woman, living in shadow, who could not bear the weight of her own heart – my heart, sunk as stone, silt cradled at the bottom of a lake.

It was easy to live in that place for all those years. I had eroticized myself as unbreakable: beyond the reach of any lover I lay with, protected. Fiercely independent, I was a girl who could accelerate from 0 to 140 in ten seconds flat, a good-time girl who left them wanting more.

When I started to want more for myself, when that lake became too murky to navigate, I wrestled with the big lie that had become the bedrock of my gender, my desire, my whole self: *I am unbreakable. I am not broken.*

x. STONE CUTTER
Medusa, Triple Goddess, was raped. She was so angry that she transformed her hair to serpents to repel those intending harm, and to serve as warning. Only those with ill intentions were turned to stone.

xi. GEM
How does Medusa kiss? Eyes open.

Skin to Scar

If you look at me carefully, you'll see that my face is asymmetrical. My nose is clinically described as a deviated septum, my mandible and maxilla aren't perfectly lined up, and x-rays show that my chin is connected to my jaw with wire. I'm a head trauma patient and a beautiful one at that. A beautifully built woman – I have the doctors to thank – six surgeries and ten years of orthodontic treatment later, compliments of the Ontario Medical Plan and the University of Toronto's Faculty of Dentistry.

No one would notice unless looking carefully, and most people don't look carefully at anything for fear of offending. My scars are practically invisible, but I don't need them to be. This face was rebuilt.

†

"Okay, Anna, we're going to give you some gas and it's going to relax you. It's going to be okay. You're going to look beautiful, just beautiful. Are you ready?" The surgeon spoke very matter-of-factly. "It's a risky surgery – like taking apart an Oreo cookie. When you separate the wafers, occasionally they crumble." He grimaced briefly. "We are operating in a very sensitive area and sometimes it takes the nerves up to two years to regenerate and become functional. You may only regain twenty to forty percent sensitivity in your lips and chin. Nerves are touch and go. On the other hand, it could go smoothly and you'll look beautiful, just beautiful. Anna, are you ready?"

I imagine a cookie crumbling and ponder the possibility of not being able to feel a lover's lips on mine.

"Yeah, I'm ready." I am sixteen years old, and this is my fourth surgery. I have settled into a stoicism that leaves me no room for reluctance.

"Okay, when I put the mask on your face start counting back from 100. I'll count with you. 100, 99, 98, 97, 96, 95. . . ."

I come to several hours later on a stretcher in the rescue position – my left arm is extended up over my head and my right arm and knee bent. I am met with familiar smells: the corked smell of ammonia, bottled piss, latex powder, antibacterial hand wash. I hate hospitals with a passion, but the rhythm of these buildings has become familiar, and in this familiarity, there is a strange comfort. I know the mechanics of this theatre; the characters and their roles, the sound and lighting elements, the church-like, holy quality of a dark house, and the drift into hyper-real, suspended time when the audience is seated and the house fades to black. I don't want the rigour that comes with playing the main character in this morbid production – I want to go away, go under again. A nurse is standing over me, just inches away from my face. Her eyes are as big and blue as the moon, and her nose appears disproportionately large. The rest of her face is out of focus.

"You did really well. You're going to be okay."

I try to move my flaccid muscles, but the room shakes violently as I tilt my head ever so slightly. I close my eyes again.

"I know you want to move, but you can't. Just try to relax. Take it slow. Do you hear me?" I blink in response, hoping to quiet her loud words "Listen, you can't move because you might vomit and that could be fatal. You need to stay in the rescue position, Anna."

"Mmmm." I mewl. My jaw had been separated and reconnected.

"Are you in pain?"

I blink.

"I can't give you anything for the pain yet – you need to come out of the anaesthetic first."

I close my eyes in self-defence. *If you can't help, then why did you ask if I'm in pain?* The exhaustion, sweet as blistering summer heat, takes me. I don't have energy to hang on to my anger. Float out to a landscape of soft shapes and muted colours. When I come to, my sense of time is adrift. *How long was I gone for? Where did I go?* The lights aren't as bright, the pain is sharper, and I have new appendages. An IV trails from my left forearm, and another tube is hanging out of my nose – I think it goes into my stomach. A third tube rests between my legs, this one to piss through. The surgeon appears.

"Congratulations, Anna. The surgery went well, really well. You'll feel better in no time, no time at all. The nurses will take good care of you." He squeezes my shoulder and disappears behind the faded brown curtain.

I try to speak, but I can't open my mouth. I want to tell him to keep his hands off me. I want to ask him why he says everything twice. And I want to know why everyone keeps telling me I'll be okay. I close my eyes again, digest the fact that this man has just cut me open and put me back together again.

When I say I was rebuilt, I truly mean rebuilt. Bone by bone. Muscle to tendon. Skin to scar.

†

With early puberty, the bones in my face shifted radically, and swiftly. I couldn't chew food without difficulty because my jaw was far out of alignment, and sleep was wrought with my own laboured, suffocating breath. Six years of a dizzying schedule of medical and dental appointments ensued, with a frequent rotation of new doctors and interns. I was finally assigned Dr Spiro at the Faculty of Dentistry who, unlike the other doctors, didn't continue with treatments that yielded no positive results. He ordered new tests and x-rays and surprising information emerged – my bones were shifting because of skull fractures, like earthquake fault lines that weren't visible. I was fourteen years old. What had caused the skull fractures?

I am a red dress

Dr Spiro scheduled a consultation with my mother and me. He asked my mom, "There must be some reason for the fractures. Do you recall if Anna was in an accident?"

She looked at me, and then down at the floor.

"Mrs Camilleri, did something happen that we don't know about?"

A few tears started to roll down my mother's cheeks.

He pressed on. "I see that this is hard for you, but any information you can give me will help us to help Anna. Mrs Camilleri – Vierra, is there something you need to say?"

My mother's voice was small. "Anna fell."

"When did she fall?"

"She was a baby – maybe a year, a year and a half old."

"Can you say more?"

She was silent for what seemed like forever and then looked up. "I went out to get a few things and when I got back to my parents' house, Anna was screaming. Her face was covered with blood."

"What happened?" I asked. I hadn't heard this story before.

"I don't know. I don't know anything else. I took her to our doctor – he said babies have milk bones, he said there was nothing to worry about."

"Mom, who was in the house when I fell?"

Silence.

"Mom, was my grandfather home – was he there?" She started weeping. "Did I fall, or did something else happen?"

She looked blankly at me, tears rolling down her face. I

slammed my fist onto the desk. Metal instruments scattered onto the floor, sounding like chimes.

After that day, I asked my mother the same questions but in different ways, and I also asked new questions. I spoke with my father and my grandmother too, but they didn't have answers for me either. No more information came, and I stopped asking. The story became another well-worn blanket of silence in my family's closet. At least, it became clear that surgical intervention was needed.

Every summer during my high school years, I entered a cycle of surgery and recovery. I returned to school each September with a slightly different face and a profoundly changed sense of myself – as both mortal, and unyielding.

After the jaw surgery, my mouth remained wired shut for eight weeks while my bones and muscle knitted together. Everything I ate during that time came from a blender, and was drawn up through a straw. Eating was an exercise in frustration without gratification or pleasure. I lost thirty-five pounds, and with every pound that melted away, at least two people commented on how great I looked. I had never received so much praise for having done so little, for disappearing into a too-thin version of myself, for being so hungry I could have chewed my arm off. This smaller and literally silent version of me was considered beautiful. That turns my stomach more than any of the tasteless concoctions I ingested during that time. I was angry with a world that would rather I be small than well, that would rather have me silent. I told people who said stupid things to me during that time to fuck off, knowing that they wouldn't be able to make out my muffled words, but they would smile and nod anyhow.

I needed the surgeries, and there were, as the doctors would say, "cosmetic benefits" which seemed to excite them more than anything else. I remember the calculated look in the eyes of surgeons who saw me the way an architect might view a partially constructed building: *Lovely foundation, it's a shame that it's not finished.* They saw me as deficient, potentially beautiful. And what greater gift could a doctor give to this world than one more beautiful woman?

I was to them the mythic frog prince, the raggedy chimney sweep turned Cinderella. I could hold this story close to my breast, hide it, and no one would ever know. My scars, after all, are quite invisible. According to the tale, the prince never spoke of his former life as a frog and Cinderella never told of her life as a servant. This is part of the magic of fairy tales. The transformed heroes or heroines assume new identities while keeping their secrets to themselves.

Forsaking a life of experience in exchange for a new life doesn't seem like a great deal to me, but I didn't make a deal with anyone to forsake myself and become Cinderella. This tale is mine to tell, freely, and without shame.

I grew these bones myself, muscle to tendon, skin to cheek. I pushed myself into this world, and this is magic.

Sorority

After I filed sexual assault charges I sat in my Vancouver apartment waiting for the first long-distance phone call from home. Then it came. It was my mother. I held my breath. She choked out her words between gasps: "I'm proud of you, Anna." This was the first time she had said that to me. I scrambled for a roll of toilet paper to mop my face. She asked if I was okay. I said yes. I lied.

We had played our parts so well, so fully; she, the wretched, unloving mother, and I, the scrappy, unlovable daughter. We had been far apart yet moving in tandem all along; afraid of touching each other for fear of seeing our own reflections, of the shame that threatens to pour down like a dark, open sky every time we look into each other's eyes. I step closer.

"I feel shaky, but I'll be okay. Are you okay, Mom?" She assures me, "I've managed for this long," then drops her voice to a whisper. "I'm sorry, Anna. I wish I could have done something. I was a terrible mother. I'm sorry, I'm so sorry." My throat tight, I whisper, "Mom, Mamma? Listen to me. It's not your fault."

During the criminal investigation that followed, I spoke with investigating officers every second day for an entire year. Family members were interviewed and no one was without opinion – some were quick to condemn me for supposedly exaggerating or lying, for digging up the past, or for lacking compassion by laying charges against an old man. Medical records were examined; the report that my family doctor was required to file by law had not been filed, but his notes provided an irrefutable historical record. Then, new stories emerged: two of my grandfather's sisters, who were estranged from our family, disclosed to interpreters that my grandfather had also raped them when they were children. Every scrap of my life, of my family's life, was catalogued.

But none of this, as grueling as it was, prepared me for the mother lode. During a conversation with the lead detective, he told me that following his interview with my mother, she called him and disclosed that she too, had been raped by her father, my grandfather. This was the first time she had told this story. In the same breath, he expressed concern for her: "Your mother isn't doing well – you might want to call her."

Anger erupted in me like molten shards. Numbers, days, years flashed around me like firecrackers. Far from being alone, I was a part of a secret sorority of blood-related women who had all been raped by the same man. I wanted to yell at my mother: *Where the fuck were you, Mom? Why did you let him near me? You knew he would come after me. It's not like there weren't any signs. I barely said a word until I was twelve. You remember those pictures I drew, don't you? Stick men with huge penises. I was so small in those pictures. I remember throwing fits, screaming and crying, "I hate Nonno. I hate him. I don't want to see him."* But she never asked me why. Maybe she was afraid of the answer. Maybe she already knew.

I desperately wanted to avoid the complicated web that I could no longer step around: my mother had direct knowledge and experience of my grandfather's proclivity for raping female children in the family. Why didn't she protect me? This question had previously been alive for me, but it took on a new acuity.

My mother believes things are straightforward, cut and dry – no Saturn returns, no Mercury in retrograde, no crossed stars, no false hope. I wanted to ask her, "So what about it, Mom? If there are no greater forces at work, truth is absolute. I've knocked myself out trying to figure this out. Tell me the truth." I imagined her drifting away onto a raft of TV shows and celebrity gossip that had long been a place of escape for her. She loved the movie *West Side Story*.

"Maria was so beautiful. Sang like an angel," my mother says wistfully, looking into the distance.

"Did you know? I need you to tell me."

"All she wanted was to be with her boyfriend. A little happiness." She drifts further, unreachable.

"I need to understand why it happened."

"Natalie Wood – Maria in *West Side Story* – she died in the water. Drowned. She was still so young."

"I heard all of you upstairs at the kitchen table, eating and talking. I thought you could hear me and just didn't care. When I went downstairs to get tomatoes, wine, or pop, I tiptoed so Nonno wouldn't hear me, but he always did. Like a wolf at the door."

I am a red dress

"Drowning must be the most terrible way to die. The water, heavy, your body, heavier. And all that time, splashing around, knowing you're one breath closer."

"When I didn't come up after a couple minutes, didn't you wonder where I was?"

She looks at me with new eyes. "I didn't know."

"Maybe I slipped and hit my head," I said.

"I would have killed him."

"Maybe I was sick in the bathroom."

"I know it wasn't enough, I know, but I made sure you were never alone in the house with him. I was always there . . . but so was my mother."

†

My mother always said, "When your grandfather dies, I'm going to the funeral in a red dress." I didn't ask her why she made this proclamation as often as she did, or what it meant to her, until very recently.

I held my tongue, and I listened to my mother tell me about the depth of her hate for her father, how ill-equipped she felt for marriage and motherhood, how unhappy she was, and how she couldn't imagine it being any different without disrupting a semblance of balance she had reconciled herself to. She told me about the many days she went to school only to fall asleep at her desk because she never slept at night. When she failed two grades it didn't occur to her that children who aren't safe, who aren't well-fed and well-loved, have other things on their minds besides long division and grammar; she just thought she was dumb. She dropped out of school before graduating from the eighth grade, and her father was the first to tell her she wouldn't amount to anything. Whenever I asked my mother for help with homework, she always directed me to my dad, saying, "Your dad is the smart one, Anna, not me." And when my brother or I did well at something, my mother said, "You take after your father – at least I gave you a good father."

She told me stories of women she knew who had been put out on the street because they had dared to speak about the violence in their lives. I listened to my mother tentatively raise questions about whether her own mother had known of her father's frequent visits to her bed, and heard her swiftly double back, and conclude that her mother could not have known.

I felt, perhaps for the first time, the depth of my mother's pain and fear, and a sympathy for her that was not erased by my feelings of anger and betrayal.

"You know how Italians are – wearing anything but black to a funeral, to my father's funeral – now that would be a disgrace. A red dress is for parties, for celebration – and I wanted to see him in a box, ten feet under. But you know something, I was sad when he died. Can you believe that? I was sad to see that good-for-nothing man go."

All those years, a part of me didn't want to hear what she had had to say about the red dress. Now I listened.

Handing Down the
Red Dress

For the first sixteen years of my mother Vierra's life, she knew desperation. Her father, Ernesto – my grandfather – pushed the door open at three o'clock in the morning, when her three younger brothers and mother lay in their beds. His belt was already undone. His motivations were clear. As he had done since she was five years old, he came, with a broad grin running the width of his square face. She lay still in bed, pretending to be asleep or dead or away somewhere. She had became so good at going away that it didn't require much effort and, really, she was no longer pretending. She spent most of the time "away," separate from the rest of the world, and everyone in it.

That night, she forced herself to stay in her body, to feel the rage and fear that she usually hid. She forced breath and life into her bones. She had grown tired of being imprisoned in her body, of the echo bouncing back, of the weight that bore down on her not only at night when everyone was fast asleep, but always.

Ernesto staggered in the doorway like a drunken bull and hesitated, as if to announce himself. She witnessed this entrance dozens of times. Sometimes she imagined him col-lapsing from a sudden heart attack, or the chandelier falling, swiftly and efficiently cracking open his skull, or a lightning bolt striking him dead. None of this ever happened. Like clockwork, he appeared in her doorway, as he had done ev-ery week for seven years. No catastrophe would stop him from coming; nothing had.

My mother was long past wishing for her mother and brothers to hear, for someone or something to save her. She had taken to sleeping with a kitchen knife, tucked safely be-tween the mattress and box spring. It already had been there for one year. She was sure that no one would find it; she alone changed the sheets. She didn't intend to use the knife, in fact, she hadn't touched it since she hid it. That night, though, she needed to feel its cool steadiness in her shaky hands. He stepped toward her. Before she felt her feet on the floor, she was standing, poised and ready. He ran his hands through his peppered hair and laughed.

As surely as she found her feet, she found her tongue. "I'll hurt you if you come any closer to me . . . you're not my father anymore." The knife and her shoulders pointed squarely. "I'll kill you."

For one long moment that stretched out like all of time, they were frozen in a tableau, the silence thick as ice. She had never spoken back to him; had never so much as looked directly at him for the fear of catching the back of his hand on her cheek.

He reeled at the sight of her. At fifteen she was a fully

formed woman. He had been sure that there was no fight left in her, that she would always be his little girl. Her body, before it rounded with curves and dark hair, flashed behind his lids. He stepped back. "We'll see." he said. "Just remember whose roof you're under, *putana* – whore." And with that, he left. My mother stared into the blackness beyond the empty doorway. From that night on, she lay awake gripping the knife, just under the sheets. He didn't return to her room again.

One year later, she married my father Philip, a handsome man with green eyes, a carpet of brown curly hair, and a thick Maltese accent. On their wedding night, she returned the knife to the kitchen drawer. No one had noticed its absence.

Within a year of their marriage, she gave birth to me, a five-pound, colicky child, and two years later, my brother Johnny. My mom solemnly swore on my great-grandmother's grave that no one and nothing would ever harm us. And with that vow, the sea of silence grew.

†

1972. The counterculture revolution was in full swing: free love, peace, LSD, and harmony. My mother longed to experience life beyond her small neighbourhood, beyond tragic family stories that felt like inevitable destiny, beyond her own story. She loved music and wanted to dance into the night, to forget the stories in her bones. Sometimes, when my dad and Johnny and I were supposed to be asleep, she applied lipstick, tuned in to the top 40 on the radio, turned the lights off, and spun the flashlight around. I watched her through the door, ajar, careful not to make any noise. It was her own private disco, and she, the dancehall diva.

My mom ironed her curly hair into long, straight tresses. She wore five-inch heels and mini-skirts that made her shapely legs stretch out for days, but the revolution was out of her reach. Our home was across the street from the house in which she had grown up. She continued to tend my grandmother's house – clean, shop, manage the finances, and avoid her father. The eyes of the entire neighbourhood were still on her. "What is a married Italian woman, with kids – *bambini* – doing with those skirts and that hair? *Dio mio!*" The neighbourhood signoras sat on their separate porches, waved hello, and whispered over red geraniums in white planters. They fastidiously counted the weeks between my mother's wedding and my birth. According to Signora DiFrancesco, she must have gotten pregnant and then married to save face. Signora Luca boasted a sighting of my mother buying condoms. Signora Angeli and Signora Di Matteo crossed themselves and kissed their rosaries. Their voices dropped to a hush as she walked past with her head held high and fingers crossed behind her back; she was not going to be a shrinking violet for them. My mom knew they were whispering about her, but she also knew that gossip's wind changed quickly, and fiercely. Next week there would be a new scandal, and she would be just another woman trying to make ends meet.

†

I am a red dress

1977. My mom listens to the radio while chopping vegetables and imagines prancing around like a gazelle in a beautiful dress while swirling ice cubes at the bottom of her tumbler. Her handsome lover replenishes her drink before dashing out the door to close a big deal. The DJ interrupts the countdown. "I have some shocking news, people. We just received a bulletin. Elvis Presley died today at the age of forty-two. . . ." Her tears fall onto the cutting board. Johnny tugs at her pants.

"Mommy, why are you crying?"

She wipes her face with the back of her hand. "Mommy's okay. The onions make my eyes water."

"Then why do you cut them?"

"They're good for you. Now go play with your sister. I'll call you when lunch is ready." My mom loved Elvis. He came from a poor family, but he had made it. Just like my grandmother always said, the good die young.

The school bell sounds. She kisses us at the door and calls out after us as we run down the driveway to the school next door, "Come home right after class . . . and don't talk to strangers. If your grandmother comes to pick you up, give her a big kiss, but come straight home. I don't want you there alone. I love you. Be good." She tidies the house, sleeps for a couple of hours, and then goes to work.

She walks through the security gate and punches in exactly on time, and checks in her purse. She is never late for work, but she sure as hell is never early. Some of her co-workers arrive half an hour before their shift for coffee in the cafeteria. My mom thinks they are crazy – like being sentenced twenty-five to life, and then showing up early to make a good impression. As far as she was concerned, her supervisors could kiss her Italian ass.

She changes into her white knee-length jacket and a white cap. She picks out defective chocolates on an assembly line that moves too fast. She isn't planning on staying at the factory longer than she needs to, but she worries; some of the other women on the line have been doing the same job for twenty years.

At the end of the shift, she deposits her uniform into a large hamper, washes up, and applies a fresh coat of lipstick. She stands in a long line with the other workers for the routine security check before leaving. On the bus, she finds a seat at the front, where the blue-hair ladies usually sit. Her body throbs from head to toe. Someone near her scans stations on his portable radio. A crackly voice reports, "Women rally at Queen's Park today for equality and choice. . . ." She nearly jumps out of her seat. *Equality and choice in what,* she thinks, *a burning bra? My bra is the only thing that holds me together on a Monday. They should step into my sweaty boots for a day. . . .* The driver chuckles. "They're nothing but a bunch of dykes, eh?" he says, but she doesn't respond. The next stop is hers.

†

I am a red dress

1987. By the time my mom quits the factory because of re-lentless sciatic pain, I am seventeen years old, and every bit as hot-tempered as her.

"Anna, don't dry the dishes with that towel. I used it to wipe the counter. Sit down." She pats the brown vinyl chair. "Do you want some espresso?"

"No, I'm going out." I glance at the clock.

"Just sit for a minute. Where are you going?"

I slide into the chair with a huff. "A meeting."

"What meeting? School?"

"I told you already – the International Women's Day com-mittee." Two years earlier, my high school English teacher had introduced me to Audre Lorde's *Sister Outsider*. I read the book forward and back and carried it around with me all winter. For the first sixteen years of my life, I also knew des-peration, and Ms Lorde's writing propelled a current of hope through me. That spring, I saw her words, "Your silence will not protect you," on a poster for the International Women's Day march and for the first time, I marched.

My mother clicks her tongue. "Oh, that group."

"It's a collective, Mom."

"What do you mean, collective? Isn't there a boss or a leader?"

"No, it's a collective."

"Well, it sounds disorganized to me, no leader, no bosses – just a bunch of women talking. How do you get things done? Anyway, I'm worried about the free work you're doing. Can't they pay you?"

103

"Mom, it's volunteer work. Feminist volunteer work."

"Feminist or not, it's work. Don't feminists need money? Don't you want to be paid?"

"It's volunteer. That means no money."

"I know what volunteer means, I used to volunteer on your school trips sometimes. Remember?"

"No."

"Oh, come on, Anna! That was only a few years ago. You're not old enough to forget things."

"I forgot."

"Okay, so you forgot. Listen, those feminists keep calling you to do more work, and they're rude. Don't even say hello. How much does it take to say hello? If they can find your number, they can find money, or do they only pay the ones with initials after their names?"

"I have a job that pays. And you know what, Mom? You can't always be paid for what's important to you." My words are clipped, enunciated. I stand up and reach for my bag.

"Don't you talk to me in that voice!" she says sharply. "I've heard enough of that in the factory to last me a lifetime. And why do you think you have all that goddamn time to run around doing free work anyway? Have you thought about that? I haven't asked you to pay any bills, have I?"

"No, Mom, you haven't asked me for a thing. I have it made. My life is bed of fuckin' roses!"

"Don't raise your voice in my house!" She slams her hand on the table, and coffee splashes onto her blouse. "See, look at what you made me do!"

"You know what? I'm tired of being your pain in the ass." I rifle though my bag for a bus token. "You won't need to make any more sacrifices for me 'cause I'm moving out!" I had been planning the move for a few months, but hadn't found a way to tell my parents.

"You're what?"

"You heard me. I'm moving out. I've been saving my money." I turn the doorknob.

"Well, leave then! Let me help you pack your bags if you're so independent! Leave me! Just like a *mangia cake*. Go!"

I stormed out of the house, and my mom didn't chase after me; hands folded in her lap, lips pressed tight. Was she afraid that if we started to talk, everything would spill out indiscriminately? Where would she start? Would she tell me about the nights her father came to her room? Would she tell me that she hadn't had a good night sleep since she was five years old? No, it was too much to sew together on a thread. Too many years had passed. Too many expanses of silence to bridge in a moment. True to my word, I moved out the following month.

My mother had only wished for two things: the winning lottery ticket and her father's death. But my grandfather continued to live, as did her memories. She had one recurring dream that she dreamt both at night and during the day: her father suffers from a painful illness and dies. No one goes to the funeral. Not one tear is shed on his behalf. Everyone, even the priest, is happy to be rid of him. When the casket is lowered into the ground, she is sitting on a stool in a jazz bar, wearing a gorgeous red satin dress, sipping scotch. Men tell her she looks beautiful, and offer to buy her drinks. She says, "No thanks, I'm buying my own," and abruptly looks away, clearly ending the conversation. Very Sophia Loren, very in control, very sexy.

The day I left, my mom stood at the kitchen sink where she looked through the living room and into my bedroom. I felt her eyes but I didn't look back; I gathered up a few photos and clothes that I deposited into a garbage bag. At the kitchen table, my dad pressed his hands tight to his ears; like the sea, his shoulders heaved up and down between sobs. Johnny was sitting on the couch, glaring at me. He shouted, "You're just gonna fuck off and leave me here? You know what they're gonna be like when you go? We're your family, you know, Anna? Family. Doesn't that mean anything to you?" Johnny's words banged around in my head like tin cans fastened to a speeding car. He kicked the coffee table over, sending the coasters and crocheted doily flying across the room. Something in me tore. I remembered the schoolyard bullies who picked on him and how I shielded him with my body. Then, when he was twelve, he waved me off and told me that he needed to fight his own fights. I wanted to say something that would make the moment better, but I was only propelled toward the door more quickly.

Keep walking, Anna, I thought as the screen door clicked behind me. *Keep walking*. But they weren't easy steps. I loved my family more than any of them knew, and staying wouldn't have changed anything; I was already gone.

Later that Saturday, they would clean the house, but for now, there was no later or earlier; everything seemed to gather in this moment like dew on a petal: there was my beautiful mother, my good father, my baby brother, behind me. I wonder if my mother thought about how quickly the years had flown by, how so much and nothing had changed. My father had become thicker around the middle, and his hair had grown thin with deep points at his temples. Johnny was still skinny, but he didn't look like a boy any longer; his voice dropped and he had seemingly sprung up overnight. I was the spitting image of my mother ten years earlier – a mane of hair down past my shoulders, eyes that flashed like lightning, an easy yet guarded laugh, and a walk that placed me firmly on the ground.

Daughter

I went to where the wind lives –

I put my ear there.

I went down below.

Where the wind lives is chaos;

what the wind does is blow.

— JUDY GRAHN

Lexicon of the Red Dress, part 3

L ike a string of goslings, my grade two classmates and I were marched off to St Nicholas of Bari Church for our first confession. We sat in hard wooden pews in the dim light, fidgeting and giggling while we each waited for our turn in the confessional – our teacher's finger pressed tight against her lips, shushing us. When it was my turn, a man I knew to call Father motioned me to follow. He wore a long brown robe and his hair parted sharply at the side. I stepped inside the room and the Father closed the door behind me. The room was empty except for two rust-coloured, vinyl chairs. He sat down across from me. "Do you have any sins to confess, my child?" he asked.

Sin, as I understood it, meant my badness. We had been taught that confessing our sins would wash them away, except for Original Sin. "I didn't listen to my mother," I offered. "I hit my brother. I didn't do my math homework, and I failed the test."

"Do you have any other sins to confess?"

I blinked back at him. "No, Father, I don't think so." I looked down uncomfortably. "I could be better, I could pray more." I hoped my words would satisfy him.

"Do you ever touch yourself?"

I fidgeted in my seat and shook my head.

"Do you ever let anyone touch you, down there?"

Did he see what was in my heart? I tried to wipe my mind clean, but images of my grandfather – his hands on me, stubble rough against my skin – flickered behind my eyes, and I heard his words: *If you ever tell anyone, I will take you to the hospital and have you sewn up. You are nothing but an ugly, dirty girl.* I folded my hands, tried to look honest, and replied to the priest my best level, "No."

"Do you ever look at picture books – dirty magazines? Do you ever touch yourself?" I was sure that the priest was no messenger from God and that I needed to get out of the room as quickly as possible. I pulled my braid around and twisted it nervously.

"No," I said. He slumped into his seat with disappointment.

I rejoined my classmates, thankful for the dimness. I was no stranger to hateful words, or my belly turning itself inside out. Priest or not, he was nothing new. I made my own covenant with God. I promised God I would hold onto to myself as best I could, until I could wrest myself free. I didn't believe that horrible things were an act of God. I believed in right and wrong and that people do bad things because it's what they have chosen.

Some things have no place in this world. Some things deserve to be sent out of this world, or at the very least, put back to where they came from. That priest, saying the things he said to me, was wrong, and my grandfather's hands had no business with my body.

The shame that I carried around with me was not mine to own. I wanted to return it to its rightful place. My grandfather would have had me believe that his behaviour was inspired by an inherent unlovable quality in me, but I had done nothing to deserve what he had done.

After hearing my mother say a hundred times over, *when your grandfather dies I'm going to the funeral in a red dress*, I conjured her, the woman in the red dress, her hair the colour of night. When I was hurting, I wondered what she would do in my place. She became a muse in my life, as real as anything – an angel, a siren, shining a light in the dark corners of my soul, insisting it is possible to live without leaving myself behind, that more than it being possible, it is necessary. It was she who started me thinking it was not enough to only get by, to try to make peace with events that are not reconcilable.

When I was thirteen, I made a promise to myself that has radically changed the course of my life. I imagined the woman in a red dress, and I made a covenant, not with God, but with myself. I vowed that the violence that has been alive in my family for generations would end on my branch of the family tree; I would not surrender to it. I could not resign myself to believing that the violence I had lived would fade into the background of my life – that the passage of time would somehow miraculously heal me.

I worked in the violence-against-women-and-children movement in my late teens and early twenties. In downtown shelters and drop-in centres I prepared meals, interpreted mail for women who didn't read English, and kept a straight face when it mattered by telling bold-faced lies (called advocacy work). It wasn't uncommon for abusive husbands to file missing person's reports, and for local police to call on their behalf, quoting details from the missing woman's file. I often wanted to say, "What makes you think she's missing? Maybe she left for a good reason."

But I mostly listened and I often felt rocked. It was there that I learned that my story, while deeply personal, is much, much bigger than me. I am not alone; none of us – women and men – who have been raped, as children or as adults, is alone. Violence is cyclical, and any so-called incidence of violence is never isolated. I have spent years working to untangle myself from its monikers: denial, self-hate, shame, silence. I am sure that I will never be done. It's the work of a lifetime. Sometimes many lifetimes.

My grandmother, my mother, and I – none of us were ever allowed to be children, not in the true sense of the word. Our lives are etched by immeasurable loss. Despite my experience, perhaps because of it, I try to live a life rooted in the values and principles I hold dear; I've committed myself to not forsaking my grandmother and my mother. Laying greater blame for the brutality I've experienced at the feet of the women in my family and then walking away from them would be untenable. They need my compassion, not my hate.

I am a red dress

I am my mother's first-born child, a daughter, and I can only imagine the covenant my mother made to keep herself safe.

My mother is my grandmother's first-born child, a daughter, and I can only imagine the covenant my nonna made to keep herself safe.

I have wondered what it would have been like to live with a wolf; to have a wolf for a father, a wolf for a husband – a wolf who has an appetite for his own.

I have had a wolf for a grandfather, but I am not Little Red Riding Hood. I am a woman in a red dress, insisting it is possible to live without leaving oneself behind, insisting that it is necessary.

Incarnadine

Wind blows cool through the side door. From my place on the stage all I can see are smoke curls dancing in the light of the stage lamps overhead; the audience, an indiscernible echo. I hear laughter, whispers, and programs fanning sweat brows.

Words roll out of my mouth; the undertow pulls me away. Today my grandfather was sentenced to three years in a federal penitentiary. *No, don't think about that.* I've wandered far from shore. The audience is a ship in the distance; I swim upstream like incarnadine salmon, break through the surface to the stage, the heat, my final words. I follow the applause off stage where the air is cooler, where there is room to breathe. Where I can swim without measuring distance.

Today my grandfather was sentenced to three years in a federal penitentiary. *No, don't think about that. Think about the list with sub-lists that waits on the desk.* I'm moving back home to Toronto in ten days. Three thousand miles away. The garage sale is tomorrow, and I'm selling all of my things. How many times have I done this?

I'm an expert at packing, having moved more times that I can count. There was always a good reason to move

— negligent landlords, crazy neighbours, expensive utilities, relationship break-ups, the need for a new view. There's a rhythm to the ritual of sorting, packing, unpacking, like the moon's cycle. Moving is not just an activity, it's an art that requires the right tools: Xacto knife, packing tape, newspapers, rope, garbage bags, a multi-head screwdriver, Allen keys, waterproof markers in at least four colours, blankets, boxes (liquor store boxes work best), and most important of all, an organizing principle.

Do you want to pack by item, room, object size, most to least used? I like packing by room with an alternating pattern: three living room boxes, then three bedroom, one bathroom. I save the kitchen for last because it's my favourite room to pack. Label your boxes. Colour code them if you're visually oriented. Wading through twelve boxes to find latex gloves at three in the morning is not sexy.

I appreciate the weight of a full box. With each move, I discover forgotten letters and embarrassing photographs. Everything old is new again and everything new is old enough to be packed. Bare walls, a fresh start.

In my different locales, there have been many lovers, new neighbours, garage sales. Nobody asks me what I am running from. Nobody ever asks me if I am running from something. On crowded buses, when a stranger's elbow is up under my chin, I ask myself this question, and I always come to the same answer: I'm running to, not from, and I hold fast like a swimmer gripping a raft. I swim some more. My stroke improves. I rest at the next island, dazzled by the view. It cycles like looped images, like the moon, like the seasons.

†

This morning I jumped out of bed before my lover was awake and began telling her about my dream, nudging her until her eyes were open and blinking.

"I'm sitting in a concrete yard, leaning against a fence, naked. You walk through the gate and hand me twelve smooth, whittled branches and a sea sponge. You're dressed in army fatigues. In a very business-like manner, you tell me to put the sponge inside my cunt and then to embed the branches. You explain that in case of rape, the bastard will get pricked, pull out, and run away bleeding. I spread my legs, insert the sponge and branches, and whistle into the traffic. No one notices my lack of clothing, not even you."

She sits upright and touches my face gently, distressed. "It's a good dream," I explain. "I'm not scared. I didn't wake up shaking."

When I was a kid, I had nightmares about hooded men banging at my bedroom door. I always woke just before the door was kicked through, in a cold sweat and a puddle of warm piss – my limbs stiff as a board. Sometimes I dreamt about hundreds of rats teeming, gnawing at the walls. I couldn't stand up. I lay in bed, looking up at the ceiling. The dreams hovered around the light fixture, waiting until nightfall to descend like mosquitoes. Until my breath slowed. Until I was

I am a red dress

limp and my body freshly pressed with sheet. Until my lips parted. Waiting, until I looked like a babe in a crib. Then the dreams came down like rain. Drip, drop.

†

I stopped wetting my bed when I was sixteen years old. I'd had enough of soggy sheets, and I went to see my doctor who told me I had enuresis, a common condition that is caused by emotional trauma or a physiological problem. He asked if anything traumatic happened to me when I started bed-wetting. I said no, then yes. Then the words spilled out: "My grandfather touched me." My body folded at the waist, and the room spun. I held onto my tears, straightened up, and looked at him. He leaned forward, his face screwed up in an empathetic expression.

But I didn't want his kindness. I wanted to get away from those words, and from myself. I gathered my bag and darted out of his office. I walked aimlessly through the city, convinced that everyone in the world had heard me. When I arrived home, my mother asked where I'd been. Nowhere – I said nowhere.

I stopped dreaming about hooded men and rats after I filed sexual assault charges against my grandfather. Now, I dream about whistling kettles, kinetic sculpture, and swimming in the Mediterranean.

I first contemplated filing charges when I was twenty years old, but I wasn't ready to speak the details out loud.

Four years later, I visited Toronto and took a walk through the neighbourhood I grew up in, looking for answers. I arrived at my grandparents' house, the house where it all happened. Apart from some minor exterior renovation, the house was preserved, as in my memory. I wanted to open the door, run into Nonna's strong arms, to burrow into the space between her ear and collarbone and savour the sweet scent of her skin. But I couldn't bring myself to cross the street. I couldn't run to her. Our reunion would come to an abrupt end, and silence would follow.

My grandmother knew what her husband had done to me, and she had let my body fall to the ground like autumn leaves. Those leaves, slippery, brown, and rotting, I could not cross.

†

A year later, at the age of twenty-five, I filed a sexual assault victim impact statement with the Vancouver Sexual Assault Squad. I spent two hours with a plainclothes officer in a small room, a dictaphone next to a pink and yellow plastic flower arrangement, tape heads spinning. The questions were endless:

"Now, we don't want to put words in your mouth, but we need to be able to pass information on to the Metro Toronto police. Exactly what type of assault occurred? What happened? How old were you? This occurred more than once? Exactly what occurred? Do you need a break? Do your parents know? Do you have any brothers or sisters? Do you need

I am a red dress

a break? If your grandfather were here today, what would you say to him? How do you feel? Why did you wait until now to file charges? What do you want to happen as a result of this statement? Are you employed?"

My answers were long winded, all over the map. What was the question, I asked repeatedly. What was the question? When the officer offered breaks, I didn't accept. I'm not sure that I would have returned, and I didn't want to carry the weight of this story any longer. I wanted to scream: *What do you mean by that? Isn't it obvious why I didn't jump up ten years ago to come and tell you about everything that's nauseated me for my whole fucking life? You want answers? Yeah, I have a job. I was raped by my grandfather. No, I haven't forgotten a fucking thing. I have a colour picture album. He stunk of tobacco, cheap wine, brilliantine, Old Spice. He threw my underwear clear across the room. I was five years old when he started messing with me. Still had my baby teeth. He used to talk through the whole damn thing. I don't know what was worse – the talking or the. . . . He said that everyone would think I was a dirty girl if I ever said a word. When he was done, he'd spit into his palms and press the loose hairs back into his pompadour. If my grandfather were here, I would spit in his face. Then, I would tell him there's a bill to pay – he needs to account for what he did. Once? Seven years, times fifty weeks a year at an average of two assaults a week, equals seven hundred and twenty-eight. I haven't eaten out in restaurants that many times. I haven't seen seven hundred films. I don't want to believe it.*

But I didn't unleash my anger at the officer. He's not the man who hurt me.

I signed forms to have documents released, spoke with the investigating officer three times a week. I began to feel afraid while having sex, and then I stopped having sex altogether for several months – my body frayed with memories.

Those months stretched out like a cracked prairie highway, September indistinguishable from April. The prairies are a long way from the ocean. The horizon, right at your toes. The sky so big it's heavy. The road just goes on. The view changes everything. Context is everything.

I am stubbornly proud of my sexuality. To anyone who has looked down on me from a moral high ground, I say, "I am not a lady. Never have been, don't care to be." I have flirted unabashedly. I've been hungry and demanding; I've told more than a few lovers how to pleasure me in no uncertain terms.

When my grandfather assaulted me, I was stone: cold, rigid, pulseless. When he finally let me go, I would run into the bathroom, lock the door, wash my hands and face, and touch myself. I discovered the vibrating "scalp" massager buried at the back of the cabinet under the sink, the pulse of the detachable shower head, the power of my own hands.

I taught myself how to orgasm while squatting, lying, or standing. I fantasized about heavy petting with Deanna Troy from *Star Trek*, necking with Carina who lived next door, straddling Mario, my classmate who bullied anyone younger or smaller. I learned how to luxuriate in my body,

I am a red dress

coming slow and easy. When my wrist got sore, I alternated hands. This was my revenge on the world – short of locking me up, no one, not my grandfather, not the neighbourhood signoras, no one could stop me from pleasuring myself. Every time I came, I was a little bit more alive. My grandfather had taken a lot, but not everything.

†

On the day my grandfather was sentenced to three years in a federal penitentiary, I performed in Seattle. Had I been able to click my heels and make a wish, I would have chosen to be anywhere but on a stage; I had little to give. I was not a performer that night, but a conjurer in two different places simultaneously – on-stage, and in the courtroom where my grandfather was found guilty.

I came back to my body during the last line of my monologue. The audience was applauding. I bowed, and walked off stage. I was floating somewhere above the crowd, somewhere above Seattle. I have found a place for my ability to disconnect and recreate a moment. It's true, the show must go on.

The guilty verdict ran through me, winded me like a blistering snowstorm. The bones of my life exhumed for everyone to see. But a part of me has always been here, out here, in the middle of a storm, in the middle of the ocean. A part of me is cold, untouched. And the truth is, the part of me that is untouchable should never have been touched.

What is plain to see is often forgotten, so I will say it again:

The part of me that is untouchable today should never have been touched.

And no verdict will ever change this.

Flame

Unlike other adults who warned about the links between lighting matches and blazing fires, my grade five teacher, Miss Cormack, did not speak a word about danger. While standing in the centre of the room, our desks in a semicircle, she struck a match and touched it to the wick of a candle. Flame. The smell of burning sulphur tickled my nose, a smell I would grow to love. She held a saucer over the votive. The flame flickered, and became smaller. Her breasts rose and fell with her breath. She raised the saucer higher with great ceremony. The flame grew. She then dropped the saucer on top of the votive and the flame promptly went out.

"Do you know why the flame went out?" she asked.

The room was silent. She, the powerful sorcerer; we, her adoring pupils. My mind raced with possibility: *The flame went out because she willed it to. The flame went out because it was done burning. The flame went out because it was the only flame in the room.*

"Fire needs oxygen to live, breathe, and grow. Without oxygen there is no fire. We need it to live. We also need fire. You'll learn more about that later. All in good time." Her eyes sparkled mischief.

She didn't speak to us in the manner that the other adults did; there was no condescension or frilly words ending in question marks. Her voice was hot caramel, ice, polished silver. There were rumours about her; each day brought a new one, more involved than the previous. Everything from former careers as an opera singer, stripper, spy, to her trav-els around the world where she had lovers in waiting. I'm sure (not entirely) that most of the rumours were just that – brilliant fabrications. There were no rumours about any of the other teachers. They didn't inspire them. Miss Cormack incited stories, dreams, fantasies, desire, even lies. She was the kind of woman who caused lovesickness, complete with fever, delusions, and madness. I imagined being one of her lovers, eagerly waiting for her next word, touch, glance. I had no idea what the word lover meant, but I wanted to know. I wanted to feel that deeply. Most of all, I wanted to become a woman like Miss Cormack: graceful, beautiful, intelligent, and coveted.

Miss Cormack was struck by oncoming traffic on Rich-mond Street eight years ago. She spent two days in Toronto General Hospital's intensive care unit with massive head injuries. Her last words were, "Let me go." Seeing her in a casket, waxen and still, would have been sacrilege. She did, however, love ritual – loved to create it – and I heard her funeral – complete with incense, candles, eulogies, and a cherubic choir – was the ultimate performance. But she was not the mistress of ceremony, and for that reason, I could not attend.

I am a red dress

Even at the time of her death, there were those who believed that she didn't die; that it was either a grand mistake or a staged performance. New stories emerged: that she was now a gargoyle living atop a gothic building at the site of the accident; that she absconded to Greece, where she spends her days eating stuffed grape leaves. What do I believe? I remember the day she caught me drawing a portrait of her in my lined notebook during science class.

"Is that a picture of me, Anna?" she smirked. "Well, you've given me remarkably large eyes. Eyes are interesting. The camera was designed on the original model, the human eye. Let me show you." She sketched an eye. "Here is the retina, the iris, the lens, and the blood vessels. The pupil expands and contracts to let more or less light in. . . . You can change your view of the world by squinting your eyes." I squinted at her. Her face fluttered and twinkled like the sun straining to shine through cloud cover. She laughed at me. "Oh, there is so much to learn." She looked like she was thinking of faraway places. "All I ask is that you listen before deciding you're not interested."

"Yes, I'll listen. Do you think eyes are windows to the soul, Miss Cormack?"

"Well, I suppose that's possible. It depends on your view."

To this day I remember the names of clouds because of her: cumulus, cirrus, and stratus, with variations like cumulonimbus, altostratus, and stratocumulus. My inclination towards romance could have led me to a dreary, self-indulgent belief that she lives in the heavens where the clouds are, but I know better. She's the stuff that lava is made of, not rain.

She once referred to Mary Magdalene as the whore who Jesus loved, and a shiver ran up my spine. I imagined Mary Magdalene holding his cock while he kissed her feet. The principal walked into our classroom just as she spoke those words: *the whore who Jesus loved.* The next day, a substitute teacher wearing a starched collar, a mid-calf skirt, and her hair in a tight bun instructed us to move our desks into rows and to call her ma'am.

I learned an important thing the day the flame went out: If I am ever trapped in a burning building, I will not open a window. I will be still and luxuriate in the heat for a moment. I will look toward the sky and think of Miss Cormack. Then, I will run toward an exit as fast as my legs will carry me, push through the heavy metal door, and burst into the open air.

Tough Girl Dreams

Shannon O'Hare gazed into the mirror of the girls' bath-room while tussling with her whitish-blonde hair when I stepped out of the stall. I glanced at her on my way to the sink. Her pale-pink skin appeared thin, translucent. She had slender legs, long fingers with perfectly trim nails, and fine hair that moved at the slightest air current. Her lips were narrow and stretched tight across her face like a pink gash. Everything about her was thin.

Next to her, I was thick and round – wide hands, coarse hair, thick lips, bulky muscles that roped around my bones, skin the colour of pan-fried dough, nails chewed up to pinkness.

We had never spoken to each other, but I knew her name. She was one of *those* girls, the rich ones who smelled like old and fresh-out-of-the-wrapper mixed together: wrinkled bills, lavender sachets, never-before-used sandwich bags. They all looked the same to me – narrow, pinched-up faces, match-ing barrettes, penny loafers, crisp white Polo shirts, pearl or diamond stud earrings. They moved together as a single bob-bing, giggling, hair-tossing unit, like pedigree horses, never straying far from one another. We, the new girls, called them snobs.

Yes, the new girls. Besides the fact that we were in grade

nine – the lowest rung on the high school ladder – we were the first batch of students to be there without having to pay tuition. In 1983, St Joe's Wellesley went from being a semi-private to a public school by way of a new, fully funded Catholic secondary school program in Ontario. Students in grade ten onward had paid a tuition fee, or rather, their parents had. None of us new girls would have been there if there was a bill to pay, and everyone knew it.

Busloads of us travelled from all over the city to St Joe's, each one of us carrying our parents' dreams for something they didn't have, or something they weren't. The other things that we had in common is that we grew up speaking languages other than English – Portuguese, Spanish, Patois, Polish, Greek, Filipino, Italian – and our parents worked in factories, construction sites, or cleaning other peoples houses, children, offices.

I expected one of Shannon's pals to burst into the can at any second, but no one did. There was nothing but the sound of the toilet bowl swirling between us.

I was tempted to skip washing my hands altogether to avoid being around Shannon longer than I had to be, but I could just hear her snickering with her look-alikes about how I didn't wash my hands after wiping myself, about how I was dirty. I wanted to give her "a piece of my mind," as my mother often said, just to see the indignant look on her pointy face.

Her voice came deeper than I expected, "You can see everything under these god-awful lights," she said. She wasn't fussing in the mirror any longer; instead, she leaned up against the paper towel dispenser examining her cuticles, her hands spread out in front of her like starfish. I decided she was talking to herself, and not to me.

"You really should stop chewing your nails. It'll give you arthritis."

I turned off the taps and shook out my hands. "Excuse me," I said, my voice even. I would have wiped my hands on the front of my kilt, but I didn't want her to think that she was the queen of the damn bathroom.

"Ex-cuuuuu-uuse me . . ." she replied, sarcasm dripping out of her puckered face.

I stepped in closer, signaling for her to move away from the paper towel dispenser. Any potential for idle talk had evaporated. If she didn't move, I was ready to nudge past her.

Finally, she stepped aside with a broad flourish of her arm, like a *Price Is Right* model showing off a shiny new car. I wiped my hands quickly and turned to leave, but not before I saw her pull a strand of silky hair between her lips. As I placed my hand on the door handle, she called out, "My father's a doctor." She circled the strand with her tongue. "What does your father do?" The sting of her words, the wet of her lips glistening under the fluorescent lamps, caught me upside the head like my mother's angry hand.

I turned back to her, "My father works for a living," I said coldly. "But you don't know anything about that, do you, Shannon?" I turned sharply and marched out, but not before I saw the insulted look on her face that I'd imagined in all those scenarios where I had said the right thing at just the right time. But I didn't feel victorious.

I moved quickly down the stairs and out the back door where I found some of my friends. I rifled through my bag for the Rothman I'd nicked from my father's pack, then lit it quickly and took a long haul. "That Shannon O'Hare, she's such a bitch," I said.

"Totally!" Joanne agreed.

"She ain't good enough to kiss my ass. Hell, none of them snobs are," Vernyce added.

Joanne stepped closer. "Did something happen?"

"She's just a bitch, that's all. Nothin' new."

"Yeah, that's for sure." Vernyce sucked her teeth, bringing the conversation to an end.

I wasn't eager to share the story I'd just walked out of, even though Vernyce and Joanne would have fallen on the ground laughing.

Shannon's words were meant to embarass me, and they had. More than that, I was mad at myself for feeling ashamed of the back-breaking work my parents did to keep a roof over our heads. I imagined Shannon's dad, silver with wisdom, commanding respect from patients and co-workers alike. I imagined my own dad going to work, never to be greeted with "Good morning, Mr Camilleri," a simple salutation afforded to those considered worthy of the courtesy.

Even as a teenager, I knew that some lives are regarded as implicitly more valuable than others. I was raised to stand up for myself, but also to expect nothing. My mother often said, *This lousy world owes you nothing, and if you get it in your head that something is coming your way, you'll be sorely disappointed.*

Shannon's body – the ease in her movement, the dance of her words, the light in her eyes – cut me. She moved freely, as if the world were hers, as if she didn't question the value of her own life, as if she deserved all that she wanted.

I hated how I felt in Shannon's presence, how her watery eyes unnerved me. I hated how sweet she smelled, and that I noticed. I felt the smallness of my life, the silliness of my private vindication, *I'm gonna be somebody.* Another voice followed, *Who you gonna be? A dancer? A professor? An astronaut? You gonna walk on the moon? You got stars in your head, girl, gonna break your heart.*

†

I had pleaded with my parents to let me go to Oakwood Collegiate, which was just blocks from home, but my mother wouldn't have any of it. She'd heard that St Joe's was a good school, and she wanted me to have a chance to "make something" of myself. She believed that Catholic school would provide me with a better, stricter education than secular school. My mother wasn't a practicing Catholic, but she was deeply ashamed of the family she came from, believing our people to be somehow forsaken and undeserving of God's love. My mother traced her perceived failure back to her father, who pushed her down every chance he got, and to getting married when she was just a kid herself. As far as she was concerned, men and boys were just the beginning of a dead end road, and school was the way out, the way to something better. If for no other reason, my mother hoped that Catholic high school would put the fear of God in me, scare me into goodness and clean-living. That's not exactly what she said though. She told me, "I don't want your hands cut up like ribbon, or your back so sore you can't bend to tie your laces. I don't ever want you to see the inside of the factory, or the ceiling of a hospital maternity ward at sixteen. The farther you're away from boys, the better."

Honestly, boys were the last thing on my mind. St Joe's was an all-girl, uniform school that was run with the precision of a monastery. At the age of thirteen, I already had enough religion to last me a lifetime. I didn't want to go to a school that required me to attend mass where adults moralized about this and that as though their own hands were clean – as if they didn't know what it meant to want, to want more, to lie or cheat, or feel cheated; as if we were the great unwashed just because we were young and hungry, and nothing but God could save us. It made my stomach turn. I knew that I was the only one who could save me, even if I didn't know exactly what that meant.

That encounter with Shannon in the bathroom became a touchstone for me; a seminal memory – like fragments from my seventh birthday party where my drunk grandfather hung upside down from the pear tree in our backyard singing pop tunes, my friends pointing and laughing raucously.

It has taken me years to fully understand what happened that day. When I replay the scene, I see hurt on Shannon's face, not indignation, and I had wanted to hurt her, even while desperately needing to believe that she, like me, was beyond hurt. I didn't want to be faced with her frailty; it would mean that she was like me.

At that time, I viewed the world through a stark lens of good or bad there were no in-betweens. Things were good or bad; people were good or bad. I reasoned everything this way, but more and more, nothing in my life, including my family, including Shannon, unfolded neatly according to this cosmological principle.

The last time I saw Shannon, she looked right through me – not to make a point – it seemed as though she didn't register my presence at all. The brightness in her face was gone, and she looked tired. Her eyes were ringed in mauve skin, her hair was dull, and her already wiry frame was much thinner. I wondered why she had become so small, sure that there wasn't a shortage of food money in her family. I wondered about her life outside of school, what her room looked like, what she hoped for, what she was afraid of. Shannon did not remain firmly lodged in my *bad catalogue*, and this unsettled me.

Family members, their mercurial natures, scared me. The most basic things I needed were provided, but love was not constant. Those who purported to love me, my grandfather in particular, hurt my body and my spirit in profound ways.

There was no safety for me, and I suspect that the adults in my life didn't feel safe either, especially in 1950s Canada. When my family immigrated, the words *wop, guinea, dp,* and *dago* were used routinely to denigrate Italians. None of us were safe – not at work, not on the street, and certainly not at home with each other.

Because of the violence that has been at work in my family for generations, I can't name one relative who believes that he or she is loveable, worthy of kindness, deserving of care, attention, gentleness. This is what violence does; it squeezes us down into creatures we are not meant to be, so self-loathing and fearful that it hurts too much to hope, constantly waiting for the other shoe to drop, for things to begin badly, or end badly. Moments of joy and pleasure regarded with suspicion.

This is no way to live. The scourge of violence and self-loathing has nearly taken me, and it's taken too many – too many of my family members, too many friends and lovers. With Shannon's question, *What does your father do for a living?* I felt shame, not because of my lack of material possessions, but because of the lack at my very centre. I didn't go to bed hungry, but there was a terrible poverty in my family; a poverty of spirit.

I'm hungry for a world where we love one another and ourselves, where we do not vest ourselves in beliefs that push some down and float others to the top. I'm hungry for others who have lived this scourge and dare to want much more than simply getting by. We are not meant to be squeezed down, to be fearful – none of us, and one is too many.

I cling to hope because it's the only thing that makes sense. Hope is not an idea removed from our lives; hope has calloused hands, is hard at work.

Kiss

Erin took me by the hand and led me into a building with a neon marquee overhead that blinked "The Rose." On the stair landing inside, a husky woman wearing a plaid shirt and a leather cap blocked the entrance. She told me to hold out my arms and legs. I turned back toward Erin.

She explained, "It's standard – you know, for weapons."

No, I didn't know. I was eighteen years old and this was my first time at a lesbian bar. I had just moved out of my parent's house, Erin was ten years older than me, and I was carrying ID that wasn't mine. I felt uneasy – and I didn't like being touched by strangers – but with Erin's warm breath on the back of my neck, I lifted my arms and stepped out wider to let the surly bouncer pat me down. Erin, on the other hand, just nodded.

"Hey, you just walked in," I complained.

She shrugged. "They know me here – besides, you're the new hottie at the party."

I grinned. "So?"

She winked at me. "So, I'd frisk you too."

Once inside, she asked, "Would you like a drink?"

"Sure – a Jack Daniels, no ice."

Erin nodded and I followed her to bar. My uncle Mike's

drink was the only thing that had come to mind.

I looked around while she talked to the bartender. It didn't take more than a quick glance to notice that I was one of two women wearing a skirt and neon plastic bracelets. Def Leppard's "Pour Some Sugar On Me" blared and a dozen or so women were on the dance floor. I leaned against the bar and tried to look like I fit in.

"Here you go." She handed me my drink and lit a smoke for herself.

"Thanks."

She leaned in closer. "So, what do you think?"

"Umm, it's. . . ."

"Different?" She asked.

I blushed. "I haven't been to many bars, and not –"

"A dyke bar?"

I looked down awkwardly.

"I'm just teasing you." She touched the tip of my nose. "It's quieter downstairs. Wanna go?"

I nodded.

We passed a group of women crowded around smoky pool tables, most of whom were wearing black T-shirts or zipper shirts, ripped jeans rolled to the top of their Docs, and variations on the Flock of Seagulls haircut, with long tails. Erin looked sexy with her flat top haircut and leather suspenders. The DJ's voice crackled overhead through the speakers. All I could make out was, "Wild Turkey shooters for a buck." Then the first few chords of George Michael's "Faith" blasted along with a burst of whoops and hollers

Anna Camilleri

from upstairs on the dance floor. We sat on a couch in a dark corner with my too-big-bag between us.

"Do you mind if I move this?" She pointed to it.

I nodded.

She placed it on the ground, inched closer to me, and took one of my curls between her fingers.

She looked directly at me. "I've wanted to kiss you since we met."

I flushed and shifted slightly towards her.

"Would you like that?"

Again, I nodded. Our lips met.

My body whistled like a kettle and I was transported back to the blistering summer that followed my tenth birthday.

Carina Terramodo and I both went to Richard William Scott Catholic Elementary School, now an empty concrete yard surrounded by a tall metal fence, which was right next to the aluminum-sided house I lived in with my mom, dad, and brother for the first thirteen years of my life. I knew every block and corner of the neighbourhood, the only world I knew; I had no idea that Toronto was such a huge, sprawling city. My grandparents lived just across the street, a dangerous walk that required dodging speeding muscle cars on Dufferin Street. All of my aunts, uncles, and great aunts and uncles on my mom's side of the family either lived down the street or around the corner. My life didn't extend far beyond the six-block radius I called home, and news travelled quickly over the clotheslines.

I was thought of as a somewhat peculiar child because

142

I am a red dress

I didn't want to wear dresses or ribbons in my hair. I was a flower girl five times before my tenth birthday; the first time, I was excited because all of the adults were excited for me, but after that it always filled me with dread. Being a flower girl meant standing exactly where I was told, and walking and smiling on command. It was no fun at all, but by far, the worst of it was the outfit. The crinoline dresses were scratchy, and as far as I could tell, wearing them drew attention to me – attention that came in ways that I didn't want.

I grew too fast to let out the stitching on the same dress, so each time I was a flower girl, my mom took me out for not-for-keeps shopping. In the change room, Mom would whisper into my ear, in case we were under surveillance, "We have to take the dress back after the wedding, so you can't spill anything on it, or run around. You have to be good because everyone is going to be looking at you."

I looked as stilted as one of the many ceramic statuettes Mom kept in the house, except I was a real live girl, pulling up the white polyester tights that would fall down around my ankles in bunches, over and over again. I had a special hairstyle too; instead of the usual braid down my back, my mom would brush my hair with No Tears hairspray, and finger-curl tiny ringlets that bounced on their own, whether I moved or not. The signoras called me *Principessa* – princess – or they'd exclaim, "*Che bellezza!*" while pinching my cheeks or patting my head as if I were a small dog.

I preferred to be left to my own devices, and besides the flower girl episodes, I was. I could make myself as small as a

143

button, as thin as a worn sheet, as quiet as a caterpillar; this was my special power, the ability to erase myself. My little brother, who made a lot of noise, distracted the adults; he was going to grow up to be a Romeo, a "real ladies-man, a charmer," my mother would beam. "You're going to break your mamma's heart," my nonna chided him. If my brother and I were a house, he would have been the windows and the light fixtures, and I, the beams and the walls. He was the spitting image of my mother. I looked like my father, which is another reason why I was thought of as peculiar.

My father, who is Maltese, had emigrated from Malta to Canada for work when he was nineteen; he was without family in this country, reason enough for my grandmother to regard him with suspicion. As a native Malti speaker, people around the neighbourhood said my father spoke "a strange tongue," a Semitic/Arabic language in which God is called Allah. My father also speaks Italian fluently, which gave my grandmother yet another reason to mistrust him. My father's status as "other" in my mother's family rubbed off on me; I was often told that I was my father's daughter – cut from the same cloth; we were both quiet, and the only ones with green eyes in the family.

Besides going to the same school, the other thing Carina and I had in common was that both our dads were considered strange. Her dad was a tall Croatian man with a limp and dark blue eyes. It was Carina's eyes that got me that summer.

Like all the kids in our neighbourhood, Carina and I

didn't go to summer camp or on vacations with our fami-
lies. From the last day of school to our reluctant return in
September, we all played from sun up till sundown – murder
ball, catch, skipping, sprinting, hopscotch, marbles, climbing trees. The best tree for climbing was the pear tree in my
backyard. It had many sturdy branches, and it yielded at least
five bushels of juicy pears every late August and September.

Carina was never my closest pal, but I spent time with
her now and again. The storefront that she lived in on Dufferin Street backed onto the side of our house. We spoke
to each other over the rickety wooden fence that separated
our yards, but I was a grade ahead of her, so conversations
with one another happened after school, and during summer
break.

Carina had long, suede-brown hair, and her father's blue
eyes with long, dark lashes. She also owned the only dog in
the neighbourhood, a German shepherd named Boxer who
howled like a wolf whenever a siren sounded. One day, instead of talking over the fence as we had done a dozen times,
I invited her to come over to my back yard. She scrambled
over the fence with just a minor scrape and we climbed up
the pear tree. There, we swung our muddied legs in unison,
eating ripe pears, and didn't talk about much of anything.
Sitting with her on a strong limb in the sunshine felt good.
We stayed there for at least two hours, until our small bums
were sore from the rough tree bark.

I don't know exactly how Carina and I got from that moment to the next, but I remember the kiss as though it were

yesterday. Her lips were sticky with pear juice. I placed my hands on her sun-warmed shoulder blades, and the excitement that rushed through me was like brush fire. I remember pulling away quickly and squealing, "Oh my God, if anyone saw us, we're dead." Then everything moved in double time with a slo-mo replay, like in the movies, right before the bad guys escape from the big explosion – sirens blaring overtop screeching tires. Carina looked scared. She jumped back and ran down the driveway and around the corner to her house.

I was anxious for a good month afterward, sure that someone had seen us, sure that it was only a matter of time before the sky fell in. Next to nothing happened, with one notable exception: after that kiss, Carina and I only ever said hello to each other on the way to and from school. We furtively avoided each other's eyes; there were no more conversations over the fence, or anywhere else.

I knew that kissing Carina would not have been celebrated; I would not be lovingly cajoled about my first girl-friend, or teased about whether she and I planned to marry. Instead, I was teased about Nick, who brought me flowers, and Gaetano, who used to come to the door to walk me all of twenty feet to school. I plainly told my family that I didn't like boys, and they breathed a sigh of relief, thinking that I was bookish and shy.

I am bookish, shy on occasion, and as queer as the day is long. It was with the memory of Carina's lips on mine that I first followed Erin into "The Rose" and later that same night, traced the inside of her thighs to her musky wetness. Lit by

I am a red dress

a clumsy girlhood memory, I didn't find home or experience what some describe as the final puzzle piece falling into place that night. But I found a part of myself that had waited for eight long years to kiss again – to feel my heat pressed tight to another's.

Swing

Johnny turned the key in the ignition, shifted into first, and we pulled away from the curb – my things rattling in the back of the pick-up we had borrowed from my uncle Mike. I lit a joint and rolled down the window.

"Do you have to smoke that in here?"

"Roll down your window, Johnny."

"Listen, I'm doing you a favour. It's the weekend, you know. I have other things to do besides get involved in a dyke drama."

"I'll put it out in a second." I wiped tears from my cheek.

"Jesus, Anna – it's no biggie. I don't like the smell of it, that's all."

I nodded.

We drove a few blocks north to Bloor Street in silence.

"Johnny, turn the car around. We need to go back to the apartment."

"Did you forget something?"

"No." I motioned to my lap. "I need to take her stuff back."

Johnny pulled over.

"What are you talking about – after what that bitch did to you?"

"I don't want to play the you-hurt-me-so-I'll-hurt-you-back game. I don't want to be that kind of person."

"You gonna let her walk all over you?" he shouted.

"I'm not letting anyone walk on me, including you. This shit's not mine. I just wanna take it back. If you're gonna help me, just turn the damn car around and drive."

He looked away from me, out the window.

"Listen – it felt good to leave the apartment with her stuff, but I don't want it now. Please let's just go back. . . . It won't take long."

He shrugged. "That's not the point."

"I don't want to go there alone. Have I ever asked for your help in a jam?"

He glanced at me and then out the window again.

We sat in silence for a few minutes while I chewed my nails, then he pulled the car around. Johnny didn't know the whole story. Six days earlier, I had arrived home from a seven-week trip to Malta. Before I had left, Kim and I were still new sweethearts; we had been dating for all of three months before deciding that we couldn't live apart. I had met her – along with Susan, Lisa, and a whole crew of party-hard women – through Erin, my first girlfriend; the first time I did a line of cocaine was with Erin a couple of years earlier, so I was still fairly green to the whole scene. Kim wasn't happy that I would be away for so long immediately after we had moved in together, but I had been planning the trip long before she came into my life.

About three weeks into my journey, I got a letter from

Kim telling me that she had been fired and that she had gotten herself in deep with the wrong people. I called home several times, but there was never any answer, nor did she call me back. I had a bad feeling in the pit of my stomach for the rest of the trip.

When I arrived home from Malta, I found our apartment ransacked. There were empty beer bottles and garbage strewn everywhere and the kitchen was burnt down. My ID and chequebook were missing, along with a couple of my journals, photographs, and the only piece of jewellery that meant something to me: a gold necklace from my grandmother. At night, strangers came around, pounding on the door and screaming about Kim and money and some deal. I kept the lights off after dark, and instead used a small flashlight so that no one would know I was home. Then I went to the bank only to find out that my account was frozen and all of the money I had saved – a few thousand dollars – was gone. The bank teller showed me the cheque duplicates that had been cashed. Each one was written in a different hand, and on several of them, my name misspelled. The following day, I got a call from a detective who told me that he'd been looking for me. He had arrested a woman named Lisa – the same woman I had partied with – who was carrying my ID when she tried to access a cash advance on my credit card. He hadn't been able to locate me so he put a freeze on my account.

All of this happened inside of six days. I was scared and embarrassed and I needed to move before I could deal with anything else. I called my brother because I figured he would come through without needing to know every detail. I fabricated a story that wasn't half as bad as the one I'd come home to. He nodded and then asked, "Where's Kim?" When I shrugged him off, he figured out that she had done a vanishing act. Then I told him the whole story, or at least as much as I knew to that point. He then cursed for about ten minutes and said he would sic my uncle Mike and his buddies on her. But the last thing I wanted was for anyone else in my family to get involved, or even to know, so I swore him to secrecy.

"Johnny, will you grab the boom box and the tool belt?" I asked. He huffed before picking them up.

I carried Kim's favourite leather jacket, a circular saw, and a bat that she had been toting around since she was kid. We climbed three flights of stairs up to the apartment. I put my key in the door, but it was already unlocked; I pushed it open. Inside, Kim and Lisa were sitting on the living room floor having a smoke, looking cosy. Kim jumped up, but Lisa took her time.

I glanced at Kim, "What the fuck are you doing here with her?"

Lisa answered for her. "That's none of your business, bitch." Then she reached for Kim's hand, but Kim pulled away.

Johnny jumped forward. "You're the bitch who tried to rip off my sister?"

I turned to him. "Johnny, back off. It's not your fight."

"You brought me –"

"Johnny, not now. Shut the fuck up."

Lisa piped up. "Yeah, why don't you both shut the fuck up and fuck right off?"

The room spun. I still had the bat in my hand and I held it up, ready to swing. I wanted to smash her face in, then her knees – watch her blood spill. I wanted to see tears stream-ing down her cheeks. I wanted to make her to pay – she was every asshole who had ever screwed me over, everyone who had ever hurt me. I stood there, bat raised, for a few seconds that stretched out and snapped back sharply – one part of me screaming, *Swing*, and another whispering, *Not like this*.

I dropped the bat, and all of our shoulders fell with it.

"Lisa, I'm only going to say this once. You need to leave this apartment now."

Kim motioned her toward the door. I glared at her as she left, then turned to my brother. "Johnny, will you wait outside for me? I need a few minutes with Kim."

"You gonna kiss and make up?"

I pointed to the door. "Go."

He shrugged. "Whatever," he said, and walked out.

I turned to Kim. "So?"

She looked down at the floor.

"Aren't you gonna say anything?"

"I'm sorry, Anna."

"What are you sorry for?" I wasn't going to let her off the hook so easily.

"Everything – things just got out of hand. I didn't mean for any of this to happen."

I looked at her blankly.

"You remember Simon?" she continued.

I nodded.

"I started selling for him and I couldn't handle it. I snorted half the shit I was supposed to move and –"

"Do you know what I came home to? You didn't bother to show up and you didn't even call me to give me a heads up."

"Anna –"

"No, I'm talking now. I don't have money for first and last month's rent because all of my money is gone, my stuff is gone, and I'm due back at work tomorrow to listen to other people's problems. Then you show up with that bitch. I don't give a flying fuck who you screw, but her? She was picked up with my ID. But you know that already, right? Were you waiting for me to leave the apartment so you wouldn't have to face me? You're a coward."

"Anna, I know that I can't make this right, but I didn't mean for any of this to happen."

"Oh yeah – well, what did you mean to happen?"

"I just wanted to – I love you."

I snorted. "You love me! Are you for real? I can't believe you just said that. What do you know about love?"

Tears streamed down her face. "What do you want me to say – I don't know anything about anything, okay? I fucked up, but I didn't mean to screw you over."

"Well, Kim, you did."

Kim stepped toward me, and we looked at one another

in silence. She had lost weight and her face looked gaunt, but she was still as handsome as ever. Muscles roped around her shoulders and down her forearms; I remembered her arms around me, her mouth on mine.

I stepped back. "We're done, Kim. We had some fun, and it's over. You don't owe me anything, alright? You don't need to prove anything to me."

I turned around and walked out the door. I heard her call after me, but I kept going.

The following week, I went back to the bank to find out how to get my money back. The manager told me that if I hadn't "benefitted" from the theft, then I should see a notary public to sign a sworn statement, so I found a twenty-dollar notary and signed the necessary papers. But when I went back to the bank with the statements, the manager didn't seem eager to help. I filed a complaint against the bank and I spoke with staff at the Better Business Bureau and Consumer Affairs in the hopes that they might be able to help me. After several months had passed, I received a letter from the bank's head office advising me that the complaint had been resolved and that I needed to sign a form to complete the transfer of funds back into my account.

I walked into the bank and straight back to the manager's office. His secretary invited me to have a seat. A few minutes later, he approached me, his hand extended.

"Ms Camilleri, I trust you're well today. You must be pleased that your situation has been resolved." He motioned for me to take a seat.

I am a red dress

I shook his hand briefly, but remained standing. "Well, yeah, but it took seven months."

"Yes, these matters do take time." He slid the forms across his desk. "We just need you to sign on the dotted line, and we'll be done here."

I skimmed them over. "Two thousand dollars was ripped off from my account, and I see here that it says two thousand, but I don't see the interest listed."

He cleared his throat. "Ms Camilleri, it's very unusual that a situation like this is resolved in the customer's favour, and we are pleased to help you, but interest is not applicable here."

"Well, then, I suggest you talk to whoever you need to talk to because I'm not leaving without it."

"Ms Camilleri –"

"Mr Jones, my mother took me here to open an account when I was five years old – what is that, fifteen years? I met you for the first time a few months back, right?"

He nodded.

"You didn't do anything to help me, so don't even suggest that I should be grateful. If my money had stayed right here, where I put it, it would have collected interest – I'm not leaving without it."

He stood up. "Please wait here for a moment."

He returned ten minutes later with more documents, a forced smile on his face. "You'll see that we're crediting your account with the interest."

I looked over the documents that showed two-thousand

and twenty-three dollars. I signed the papers and slid them back across the desk.

"Will the money be transferred today?" I asked.

He nodded. "Yes."

"Great. I'd like to close my account."

I left the bank with a draft note and I left Toronto a few months later.

Girls Run Circles

I am twenty years old and my girlhood is both a long gone whisper and a stone's throw away. Girlhood: the state of being a girl, innocent and unknowing, a female child. Girl: the cartography of a woman's beginning. Girl: a country I wish I could at once re-visit and forget.

I watch two girls run circles around a metal bus stop sign. The taller girl, the one with rows of neat braids tied with ribbon, is making chomping, chewing sounds – intermittent growls. The other girl, her cheeks flushed candy apple red, squeals in a high pitch at the idea of being bitten. Delighting, sparking, spinning in the exhilaration of this high-speed chase, cutting through the wind like silverfish. Round and round, summer vacation, full-sun-sidewalk merry-go-round.

They swim in each other's laughter, in each other's girlishness. In these high stakes – this-is-all-that-matters game – of predator, prey, they are complete and reckless and there is nothing else but the belly of their joy.

In them I glimpse the girl I fleetingly was. I want to take them by their small, sweaty hands, sit with them on a stoop littered with bubble gum wrappers and cigarette butts and show them where I've been and hope my words may offer some protection. Give them a story that is confounding, contradictory, and truer than any other stories they will hear. *Sugar and spice and everything nice. Diamonds are a girl's best friend. The world is your oyster.*

Give them a story that is more true, most true, true blue. I would say: You may lose yourselves. Life is about finding much of who we once were and there are many lost girls who eventually find something of themselves again. I would tell them, you are precious and special and beautiful, not because you are girls, good girls, pretty girls – just because you are.

See, girls, I would say, if you are celebrated for being pretty, then the rest of you remains unseen, if this is expected of you on your saddest days, if you are picked apart and judged for not being the right kind of girl, if you feel like the only lonely girl in the world . . . remember.

If you writhe in the unbearable tightness of your skin even as you want the eyes of strangers on you, if you learn to hold their gaze and drop your eyes to the ground when you feel consumed, if you revel in and yet are repulsed by those words, "You're a pretty girl, a good girl" . . . remember.

I am a red dress

If these words send you into a snowstorm at midnight to a 7-Eleven to buy chips, pop, chocolate bars, and licorice, then run home where you curl in front of the television set and tell yourself you aren't worth shit; if you learn to tell yourself you are unloveable because your father ignores you, your mother abandoned you, and kindnesses are far and few between . . . remember.

Then I would ask them to look back on their girlhoods, and remember that day in the blazing sun, the day they played catch around the pole. The day they found a quarter in the sidewalk crack they stepped on but were trying to jump over while playing hopscotch all the way to the corner store, and the jaw breaker they bought and passed back and forth, sticky mouth to sticky mouth, until it was just a little bump of sweet. I'd ask them to remember the heat in their bodies, the grit on their hands, the sweat trickling down the back of their necks, how their laughter filled the streets – their streets. Remember.

And if they told me they had forgotten everything, I would say, Make it up, girls. Give yourself a story that you need – even if it's confounding, contradictory. Imagine a love so fierce it brings thunder to its knees. I would tell them that life is a balance of finding who we once were and filling in the gaps with dreams and longing and the imagination of a child.

Topsoil, Aftershave, and Charm

In Vancouver, I discovered one of the local dyke hangouts: a bookstore and coffee bar on Commercial Drive nestled amongst grocery stores, billiard halls, and restaurants. I was having a smoke out front when someone in a rust-patched pick-up pulled up. She jumped out, smiled my way, and sauntered in as though she owned the joint. Her straw-coloured hair shot straight out in cross-hatched diagonals; the collar of her denim jacket was turned inside, work boot tongues stuck out from the bottom of her cords, and rumpled scraps of papers flapped out of her back pocket. I breathed in her bitter/woody/sour scent as she blew past – she smelled like the kind of trouble I liked, and that I had sworn off of a dozen times – hints of topsoil and pot, layered on top of aftershave. Coastal air, heavy with wet and tree bark and salt residue, carries a scent trail a long, long way.

I went back inside where she turned to me and offered a firm hand. "My name's Jo." Then she told me she was a landscaper and that she'd run away with the circus someday. I told her I had just managed to get my legs feeling right again after a five-day drive across Canada, and that I'd never seen mountains before driving through Alberta.

"Oh, yeah?" She rolled a toothpick between her front teeth like she was in no hurry. "Where'd ya come from, besides out of the blue?"

"Toronto."

"Oh, yeah. Big city girl, eh?" I sensed she had a lot more to say on the subject, and I was sure I would hear at least some of it before long.

"Yeah, it's a big city." The wooden stir stick I'd been nervously twirling flew out of my hand and landed in Jo's hair. "Oh God, I'm sorry!" I said. "Let me get –"

She tilted her head forward and the stir stick landed in my lap. "Thought you might want that back."

"Thanks." I set it down on the counter next to my empty mug. Thanks? I felt like an idiot. I was going to ask Jo if Vancouver was her home, but the moment was gone, which was just as well. I could hear her say something like "Don't I look at home?" and I'd respond with a brilliant one-liner like, "Yeah, sure." Then I'd bumble along with, "I didn't mean anything . . . I was just making conversation."

Jo pulled the toothpick out of her mouth swiftly as if she just remembered she had somewhere else to be. "You like stories?"

"Yeah, I love a good story." I settled on the creaky stool, telling myself not to fall off.

"A good story? Okay, I'll dial up a *good* story." Jo disappeared into the dusty book stacks. I had just finished counting the coffee grounds in the bottom of my mug when she sat next to me again, but closer this time.

"Ready?" she asked. I noticed a delicate pouch of skin that gathered in the centre of her upper lip, like a widow's peak, only on her mouth. I nodded.

Not fifteen minutes had passed since we had set eyes on each other, and I was positive the circus would find Jo; she wouldn't need to go looking. She gave me a quick wink and produced a Dr Seuss book from behind her back. She leaned in till her left shoulder and my right shoulder touched, and I watched her mouth while she sounded words with a hint of an Irish lilt. She kept focused on the page, looking up just long enough to catch my eye, and shifted in her seat. With each shift in weight or footing on our stools, we returned to contact; shoulder touching shoulder, kneecap touching kneecap. I noticed a trace of magnolia on her, of a young tree just before heavy blooms fall away.

Even before she whispered *Sam I Am* – before she uttered a word – I was sunk. Was it her rumpled collar, the way she rolled the toothpick between her teeth, coughed and read all at the same time, or the sweetness of being read a story in the middle of the afternoon, in the middle of a coffee bar with people milling around? I was love-struck.

Jo closed the book with a snap. "Nice little story, eh?"

"Yeah, really nice." I drew the mug to my mouth, and not one bitter drop wetted my tongue. "I keep thinking there's more coffee in the cup . . . I finished it a while ago."

"You wanna 'nother?"

"No, thanks. I think I'd vibrate right off the stool."

Jo smirked. "I'd like to see that." We both laughed out loud.

"Wanna blow this joint?"

"Sure." We left with at least six pairs of eyes on our backs. Apparently, Jo was the dyke equivalent to the welcome-wagon.

Jo climbed into the pick-up. There was a pile of chocolate bar wrappers and empty coffee cups on the passenger seat.

"I'll just move that out of the way." Jo stuffed the wrappers and cups in the gap between the seat and the window and wiped the crumbs away with her shirt sleeve. "There's a seat for you, my lady."

"Thanks." I climbed in.

"So, where do you wanna go?" That same smirk danced on Jo's face.

"I like surprises."

We lit smokes, and Jo popped in a tape. It was Simon and Garfunkel, which surprised me, but I couldn't say why.

Jo looked over at me. "I like a good tune."

I nodded. "When were you born?"

"'69 – year of the Rooster."

"What do you mean?"

"Year of the Rooster, you know – Chinese astrology."

"Oh." I didn't know anything about Chinese astrology.

"Roosters are supposed to be funny and hot-headed," she said.

I smiled. "Sounds like trouble. Are you?"

"Depends on what you mean by trouble." She winked at me.

"Okay . . . well, you're funny."

"Yeah, I like to think so."

"And humble too." We laughed in unison.

Jo turned up the volume and sang along, one eyebrow cocked: "Cecelia, you're breaking my heart. You're shaking my confidence daily. Oh Cecelia, I'm down on my knees, I'm begging you please to come home. Come on home."

I sang back, "Making love in the afternoon with Cecelia up in my bedroom. I got up to wash my face. When I come back to bed, someone's taken my place." We harmonized while we drove over a bridge, and then another. Before long, the trees were taller and greener. We drove around sharp bends; a wall of amber rock face was on my right, and on my left, the biggest houses I'd ever seen. And then, an explosion of deep blue.

"Is that the Pacific?"

"Sure is – pretty, eh?"

"Beautiful."

"Thought you might want to see her – wanna feel the water?"

I nodded.

Jo kicked off her shoes, and I followed suit. She took my hand and led me down into the bay. The water was icy cold, but it felt good. We walked for a bit and then settled on the cool sand.

She touched my hair. "Pretty."

I am a red dress

I reached for her mouth, gently stroked the pouch of skin on her upper lip. "I like your lips."

Jo's cheeks coloured and she leaned in closer. "Can I kiss you?"

I replied without a word. Her mouth was as soft as it looked and her tongue, velvet. She traced the skin under my chin to my collarbone. My breath caught.

"Is this okay?"

"Mmm-hmm. You feel good."

"Do you want some dinner?"

The question jarred me. "Umm, sure."

"I don't have much at my place – I can make us some tea and toast."

"Your place?"

Her face lit up with wickedness. "Yeah, my place." She winked at me. "Want some toast?"

"I'd love some toast."

At Jo's apartment, she inserted the key in the door and turned back toward me. "Just to warn ya, my place is a mess."

I nodded.

We walked around her kitchen table, stacked with newspapers and take-out food containers, and then down the hallway into the living room/bedroom. Jo cleared a place for me to sit on the coach. "Thanks," I said, but instead of sitting, I walked across the room to a cluster of black and white photographs. I pointed to a picture of a child who was standing on a dock, holding up a big fish. "Is that you?"

165

"Yeah, my gramps says that was my first catch. He's there with me but you can't see him."

"You look pretty happy with yourself."

Jo walked over to the photograph. "Yeah, I guess I was."

"And are you happy with yourself right now?" I tugged at Jo's collar.

She flushed with colour again. "Yeah, I feel pretty good."

I pulled her toward me and ran my tongue along the blonde down above her upper lip. "You taste like you smell," I said.

Jo tapped the radiator nervously. "Bad?"

I shook my head. "Good," I said. I ran my tongue along the inside of her lower lip and placed my hand on the back of her head. I kissed her deep and listened to the rhythm of her breath as it slowed and caught. I tugged at Jo's belt buckle.

She pulled back slightly. "I thought you were shy."

"Do you want me to be shy?" I teased.

Jo beamed. "No – I mean, I just thought you were."

"Right now I'm not." I pulled my top and bra up over my head. "Would you like some help out of your clothes?" I asked.

"No, I'm good right now." Jo stepped toward me. "But I like you naked." She cupped my breasts and stroked my nipples with her thumbs. I pressed my knee into her crotch and her breath came faster and hoarse.

I whispered into her ear. "I want you to fuck me." Jo took

me by the hand and led me to her bed. She pushed the hair out of my face and tongued my nipple. I moaned. She slid open the bedside table and pulled out a harness and dildo.

I reached for her. "That's not what I meant. I want your hand inside me."

We stayed in her apartment for two days before we came up for air. Sleep, food, and water deprivation, combined with a steady diet of cigarettes, coffee, dry toast, and sex caused a delirium that made us fast girlfriends – which is the wrong word, but it'll have to do.

We carried on for three months. After it ended, we nodded uncomfortably at one another from across rooms and streets for a year before we spoke again. We became friends, eventually. Thirteen years have passed since the day Jo pulled up in a pick-up and charmed the pants off me. She did join the circus, and later, ran away from it. I've driven across the Rockies a dozen times since then, twice with Jo, and I've swam naked in the Pacific Ocean without thinking, *Am I going to make it to thirty?*

That afternoon with Jo reminds me that touch is good, and that sometimes, love doesn't know its own name, but lust is sure-footed and can come swiftly and surprisingly, when you least expect it.

Prodigal Daughter

When I left Toronto, the city that had been home to me for twenty-one years, I hadn't planned to leave for good, nor had I planned to return. I hadn't planned anything except the ride, and even that was casual at best. Several people happened to be travelling west on a bread and water budget and I was among them.

I had never before seen mountains, or wide open prairie where the sky is much bigger than the seemingly endless stretch of flat land. I had not been to the edge of the Pacific Ocean, nor had I *felt* colour – explosions of green, golden hayfields, stripes of purple – flashing past our car like vertical fireworks. My body keened to change with the land – yearned to dissolve into it, to fold and rest for a while.

With every hydro pole, every kilometre, every rest station and roadside diner, I felt my past melt into the distance behind me. At least, this is what I imagined: the road absorbing my stories, the Rocky Mountains casting a cloak over my body, me, small in their shadow. I wanted to forget the stories in my bones, to be lost in a new life.

In the Book of Luke, there are three parables jointly referred to as the "lost parables": the lost or prodigal son, the lost sheep, and the lost coin. The parable of the lost son differs from the other two in that the father laments the loss of his son, but he doesn't search for him. The son left home of his own accord and returns of his own volition, so was he really lost? Assuming that the son was indeed lost, who was he lost to – his father, or himself? What does it mean to be lost, and then to be found? What does it mean to be lost to oneself?

To my parents I was, undoubtedly, their lost daughter, having left home without clear purpose. But I didn't feel lost. I was young, queer, and happy to have left a family that I felt bound by. I had no map, no compass, no coffers. I was wild with wind and sure of nothing except the need to leave the life I had known and the child I had been.

I was a scrappy child, constantly on high alert, closely observing everyone around me so that I might find a way to intervene or somehow control the violence that invariably came with the day. I escaped into my imagination. It was there that I created for myself, and found, a better, safer life than the one I actually had. I wrote stories and poems throughout my entire girlhood – my imagination is what sustained me and answered my desparation. In my rich interior life, I found new worlds to explore with characters of my making – a place where girls had the tools required for mortal combat.

Writing was my lifeline, but there was also something inherently high-risk about putting myself to paper. Much of what I wrote was autobiographical, and in my stories, I saw pain and turmoil reflected back at me, and I didn't want to have anything more to do with that reflection. Before I left Toronto, I purged. I gathered up all the writings I had toted around in string-tied bundles and shoeboxes, carried them to Christie Pitts Park in grocery bags, and made a beautiful bonfire of them.

But the thing is this: I rid myself of my writings and travelled across the country, yet I was still carrying around that runny-nosed, scared little girl, and I didn't think much of her. I had become convinced that she, as the keeper of my stories, needed to be banished from my memory.

In Vancouver, there was plenty to distract me from all that ailed me, for a little while anyway. I went about acquainting myself with the city and finding a community. I settled into the Commercial Drive area, a part of town that was akin to the area in which I grew up, a working-class Italian neighbourhood where Italian was commonly spoken.

But distance did not rid me of memory; if anything the expanse allowed me a perspective I had lacked. In a series of snapshots – my archive of memory – the story of violence I had survived was documented. I experienced a potent sensory acuity in relation to those images – sharp scent, loud sounds, bright colours – but they were also strangely detached, the same disconnect that happens for me when I watch atrocities on television. I experienced my life as an audience member, a viewer, a voyeur – located outside of the heart of my own experience, and with no sensibility for or appreciation of it.

I had not grieved for myself, for the child I had been.

I am a red dress

Somewhere along my journey, from childhood to woman-
hood, I conflated painful memories with my imagination. It
was imagination that saved me as a child, and it was the act
of beginning to write again that allowed me to see through
my own lack of compassion for myself. It was there, on the
page, that I began to find the child who had been lost to me
– a child who desperately needed her dignity restored. Filing sexual assault charges was part of a process of restoring
dignity to my life, but I hoped that it would provide me with
an end unto itself – that I would be able to close the book
on that story.

But there could be no end as I had imagined it. No matter what I did – no matter how far I ran, how swiftly or how
often, no matter how fervently I denied the shame that had
rained down on me for all of my life – I would not become
whole without grieving for my young self, and it was with
that realization that I returned home to Toronto four years
after I had left.

†

Some time after my return, I read at the launch event for a
book entitled *Curaggia: Writings by Women of Italian Descent.*
The narrow upper level of Bar Italia was filled to capacity
with Italian-descended people of all ages, mostly women,
and a good many of them lesbians. I bumped into a woman
I hadn't seen in over thirteen years, a girl from high school
named Mara. She threw her arms around me and said,

"You've become exactly who I thought you would be! I knew you were an artist."

I was taken aback by Mara's words, through no fault of her own, and they kept me on the verge of tears for much of the night. Until then, the multiplicities of my identity had been quite fragmented – in one room, I was Italian, in another, Maltese, in yet another, a queer writer. With Mara's words, all of these identities, these selves, gathered as if on the end of a pin – sharp and ready.

I had been afraid that I would be judged by folks who, while mostly strangers, felt like kin. Even though my mother tongue is Italian, and I grew up amongst other Italian Canadians, I had never felt fully accepted by other Italians because of my mixed ethnicity, and later, because of my feminism and queerness.

My sense of home isn't rooted in any one place or community – not amongst family, queers, or other artists. Points of connection existed for me in all of these places, but each location had been quite separate and apart from the others, a source of discomfort in which I had also found a degree of safety. Like so many of us whose lives have been riddled with loss, I've developed a reflex for it – I'm ready to respond to loss even when there is no clear indication that it's on the way. But I wasn't rejected that night, not by Mara or anyone else. The event was groundbreaking for me. I heard the words "Italian" and "feminist" spoken in the same breath, without derision.

When I looked back on my childhood, I remembered an

awkward, tarnished, unremarkable girl. I had nothing good
to say about the child I was. Mara's words cut through the divide I had created between the young girl I had been and the
woman I was. Disconnecting from my young self was a way
of putting distance between the tragedy of those years and
a future that seemed inaccessible. That Mara, a girl who'd
known me in those most difficult years, had seen a future for
me, a future in which I flourished as an artist, dissolved that
distance in an instant.

I also hadn't thought that my stories would be interesting to anyone else but me. I never saw a future for my stories. Any such thoughts would have been far-fetched and
ridiculous as a young person, but I wrote, and I have always
written, because I saw a future for *myself* in my stories – and
it was there that I created a place for myself in the world,
where I made sense of my experience.

Writing doesn't come easy – I work at the craft of it – but
I've spent an equal amount of time trying to convince myself
that I deserve to write, and that my writing belongs in the
world, time that I may otherwise have spent writing. At least
part of my ambivalence is based in the challenge of writing
autobiographically-inspired stories. My story does not exist in
isolation – no one's does; our histories are interconnected and
overlapping. I've been willing to navigate the deep waters of
telling a story that is only partially mine to tell because I believe in the power of narrative, and I believe that imagination
is the single most important precursor to change.

It is in the story that I find myself.

Epilogue

Writing this book was preceded by recurring dreams that I had over a period of four years. I dreamt of a woman wearing a red gown, running down a long, wide hallway where giant ornamental chandeliers swing ominously. In another dream, the same woman is standing perfectly still in an empty, stadium-sized ballroom decorated with very ornate gold mouldings and flying buttresses. I dreamt many variations on the theme of women in red dresses, of my hands building a red dress out of tissue paper and wire, of me, or alternately my mother and my grandmother, wearing one. Some of the dreams had a cinematic quality – grainy with quick cuts and high contrast, film noir lighting; others were visual poems – unwieldy, and non-linear in structure. Each dream left impressions on me that carried me into my waking life.

It would have been reasonable to assume that the dreams, which I had come to think of as the *red dress gallery*, were manifestations of my creative life. My desire to understand and, in the words of Dorothy Allison, to "remake the world" is what motivates me.

I believe the world desperately needs remaking, and I

am troubled by our progress. With phrases like *"You've come a long way baby"* now a part of our everyday language, feminism is made a mockery of, and – this is what profoundly disturbs me – many of us believe that we live in a world that is so much better for women. That belief offers us comfort, even if it is founded on illusion. We are not free from misogyny, xenophobia, or racism, but we are free to imagine and work for a better world, and better lives.

I interpreted the *red dress gallery* as a reflection of my desire for justice and my efforts toward this vision. But there is more. Initially, I was intrigued by the persistence of the woman in the red dress, but I eventually became irritated by the frequency of the dreams. I believed that the dreams over a sustained and long period of time were a signal – a flashing red light – stop and proceed with caution, or perhaps stop, look, and listen; be open to a changing of consciousness. More than metaphor, *I Am a Red Dress* is my attempt to unravel a stirring of memory, a trace that is inextricably tied to my culture and class, and to the imaginations of women in my family, centred by the incarnate spirit of a woman in a red dress.

Prior to my recurring dreams, the stories in this book had been with me for years, and they will likely continue to be the well from which I draw. It's been said that there are a thousand ways to tell a single story, and it's been said that there is only one story to tell; I believe that both expressions reflect a truth – they stand side by side like two pillars, one supporting the other, one made possible by the other's existence. The Prologue for this book was on my lips one morning a couple of years ago and like a beacon, there came a new sense of urgency. I scratched out the words in my morning hand and the *red dress gallery* stopped opening like an iris in my sleep; instead, stories unfolded. Some of these writings are here, and others are yet to come.

Acknowledgments

Thanks to Robert Ballantyne, Trish Kelly, Blaine Kyllo, and Brian Lam at Arsenal for being wonderful to work with, and for publishing books that I want to read. I am especially grateful to Blaine, Brian, and Trish for their generous contribution to this work as a brilliant editorial team.

Thank you to Tristan R. Whiston for coming along at just the right time; JP Hornick for feedback; Leslie Davis for being certain; Bobby Noble for enthusiasm; Chloe Brushwood for understanding in ways that exceed language; Anjula Gogia for support; my long-time friend Gwen Hay for good love; Gwen Bartleman for encouragement; Ami Mattison for poetry across time and place; Leslie Peters for trips to the Goodwill; Richard Carrier Bragg for listening; Ingrid Kuran for good wishes; Adrien Whan for technical assistance; Ivan E. Coyote for beginnings, endings, and the in-between; and Quinton and Sadie for being devoted canine companions.

I am particularly indebted to Tristan and JP for listening to and reading every new scrap of writing, and for being willing to in the first place.

I gratefully acknowledge the support of the Canada Council for the Arts, and the Toronto Arts Council.

Publication and Performance Notes

Agnes De Mille. *Dance to the Piper*. New York: De Capo Press, 1980.

Lorna Goodison. "Mother the Great Stones Got to Move." *To Us All Flowers are Roses*. Chicago: University of Illinois Press, 1995.

Judy Grahn. "The Queen of Swords." *The Queen of Swords*. Boston: Beacon Press, 1987.

Audre Lorde. "The Transformation of Silence into Language and Action." *Sister Outsider: Essays and Speeches*. Berkeley: The Crossing Press, 1984.

Libby Scheier. "There Is No Such Thing as Silence." *Kaddish for My Father*. Toronto: ECW Press, 1999.

†

I am a red dress

Selections from this book have appeared, some in earlier or amended versions, in the following books and periodicals: *Curaggia: Writing by Women of Italian Descent*, edited by Nzula Angelina Ciatu, Domenica Dileo, and Gabriella Micallef; *Geeks, Misfits and Outlaws*, edited by Zoe Whittall; *Bent on Writing: Contemporary Queer Tales*, edited by Elizabeth Ruth; *Brazen Femme: Queering Femininity*, edited by Chloë Brushwood Rose and Anna Camilleri; *Boys Like Her*, by Taste This (Ivan E. Coyote, Anna Camilleri, Lyndell Montgomery, and Zoe T. Eakle); *Borderlines*; and *Tessera*.

"Compass" is an excerpt from a novel in progress tentatively titled *Red Herring in the Ring*, and an earlier version appeared in *Geeks, Misfits and Outlaws*, edited by Zoe Whittall (McGilligan Books, Toronto, 2003).

An earlier version of "Cut from the Same Stone" appeared in *Brazen Femme: Queering Femininity*, edited by Chloe Brushwood Rose and Anna Camilleri (Arsenal Pulp Press, Vancouver, 2002), and later performed at San Francisco's National Queer Arts Festival 2003 in the Brazen Femmes program.

An earlier version of "Blow" appeared in *Brazen Femme: Queering Femininity*.

Anna Camilleri

An earlier version of "House of Cards" was performed at George Brown College's 2003 Sister Fest program, and at the 2004 Seen and Heard Festival (EstroFest Productions, Atlanta) in the Slings+Arrows: Opening Voices, Healing Wounds program.

Some of the material in "Handing Down of the Red Dress" appeared in *Curaggia: Writing by Women of Italian Descent* (Women's Press, Toronto, 1998) as "Red Dress."

An earlier version "Skin to Scar" appeared in *Boys Like Her: Transfictions*, by Taste This (Anna Camilleri, Ivan E. Coyote, Zoe T. Eakle, and Lyndell Montgomery, Press Gang Publishers, Vancouver, 1998) and was performed with Taste This in 1995 in the Beggar's Feast tour.

Some of the material in "Kiss" appeared in *Summer Play* in 2004 as "Blistering Kiss," and was later performed at the 19th annual Mayworks Festival of Working People and the Arts in the Queer Verve program.

An earlier version of "Girls Run Circles" appeared in *Bent on Writing: Contemporary Queer Tales*, edited by Elizabeth Ruth (Women's Press, Toronto, 2002). The piece was first performed at the Clit Lit series in 1998, and later performed with musician and composer S. Lynn Phillips for Taste This's Too Close to Fire full-length performance and tour, and

I am a red dress

also at Queen's University, Buddies in Bad Times Theatre (Strange Sisters: Revenge of the Mudflap Girl), York University, San Francisco's National Queer Arts Festival 2003 in the Brazen Femmes program with Chloe Brushwood Rose and Michelle Tea, and at the 2004 Seen and Heard Festival (EstroFest Productions, Atlanta) in the Slings+Arrows: Opening Voices, Healing Wounds program. "Girls Run Circles" has been performed live on radio, and has been broadcast on CKLN 88.1 FM.

An earlier version of "Flame" appeared in *Boys Like Her: Transfictions* as "Sparrow." This piece was performed with Lyndell Montgomery (violinist and composer) for Taste This's Beggar's Feast full-length performance and tour, and later, at the Clit Lit series.

An earlier version of "Incarnadine" appeared in *Tessera* (Volume 23, Winter 1997), and later in *Boys Like Her: Transfictions.*

Anna Camilleri is a writer, spoken word artist, and curator who lives in Toronto, Canada. She has performed for the last decade across Canada and the U.S. in theatres, festivals, universities, and colleges. Anna co-edited *Brazen Femme: Queering Femininity* (Arsenal Pulp Press, 2002), which was shortlisted for a Lambda Literary Award. She cofounded Taste This, a spoken word performance troupe that collaborated to publish the critically acclaimed *Boys Like Her: Transfictions* (Press Gang, 1998). She has curated and directed numerous programs in a variety of media and is the Performing Arts Co-ordinator with Mayworks Festival of Working People and the Arts. Her next book, *Red Light: Superheroes, Saints, and Sluts*, an anthology that explores new interpretations of female icons, is due for release in fall 2005 from Arsenal Pulp Press; she is also working on a novel. Anna can be contacted at *annacamilleri.com*.